BACKROADS, NEW JERSEY

BACKROADS,

DRIVING AT THE

RUTGERS UNIVERSITY PRESS
NEW BRUNSWICK, NEW JERSEY, AND LONDON

NEW JERSEY

SPEED OF LIFE

To Jeffrey —

I hope you
enjoy the book

Mark Di Ionno

MARK DI IONNO

Library of Congress Cataloging-in-Publication Data

Di Ionno, Mark.
    Backroads, New Jersey : driving at the speed of life / Mark Di Ionno.
      p. cm.
    Includes index.
    ISBN 0-8135-3133-0 (alk. paper)
    1. New Jersey—Description and travel. 2. Roads—New Jersey. 3. Scenic byways—
New Jersey. 4. Di Ionno, Mark—Journeys—New Jersey. 5. Automobile travel—New
Jersey.   I. Title.
F140.D5 2002
917.4904'55—dc21

                                                    2002020157

British Cataloging-in-Publication data for this book
is available from the British Library.

Manufactured in the United States of America

FOR SHARON, MY LIFE NAVIGATOR

C O N T E N T S

ACKNOWLEDGMENTS

This book would not have been possible without the patience, and—I admit—permission of my wife, Sharon, who has endured the road trips and tolerated the lost weekends.

My children—Anthony, Michelle, Stephanie, Matthew, Mark, and Laura—too, have all been good sports, and gone along for some of the rides without much complaint. I hope they remember these trips the way I do . . . as memory snapshots of happy times.

Marlie Wasserman at Rutgers University Press deserves credit for encouraging me to break the proven "guide" format and write this book, a book with more color and feeling.

I'd like to thank many people at the *Star-Ledger* who supported this book: Editor Jim Willse, who understands the value of Jerseyana and who has always supported my ongoing New Jersey and newspaper education. Managing editor Rick Everett, who has always allowed me, in his words, to "build institutional knowledge." Writer Amy Nutt, who did triple duty as prose coach, proofreader, and ego-booster, editor Deborah Cohen, and writers Robin Gaby Fisher and Susan Todd, who all read the work-in-progress with genuine interest and encouraged me to keep going. Writer Mark McGarrity and editor W. C. Stroby, who are brothers in arms. Irv Bank, who successfully brought the manuscript in from cyberspace.

Photo editor Pim Van Hemmen and photo librarian Barbara Moss for helping me select the perfect photographs. All the *Star-Ledger* photographers whose artful work appears in this book, and Damiko Morris, the graphic artist who did the maps.

Special thanks to my two boyhood idols: the late Bernard Malamud, who taught me great stories can be spun off ordinary lives—the most important lesson I've learned as a writer—and *Star-Ledger* sports columnist Jerry Izenberg, who taught me to always write my truth—the most important lesson I've learned as a journalist.

I'd also like to thank authors John Cunningham, Thomas Fleming, and John McPhee, and the writers of the *WPA Guide to 1930s New Jersey*, who all got there before I did; Bruce Springsteen, who took Jersey road culture global; Al Stewart, whose poetic lyrics remain influential and are subliminally reflected in many of the passages of this book, and Mark Knopfler and Gordon Lightfoot for providing endless hours of driving music.

Most of all, I would like to thank my father, Anthony P. Di Ionno, for driving.

BACKROADS, NEW JERSEY

I'm a Jersey guy, through and through.

When I joined the navy to see the world, I instead got stationed in Philadelphia and ended up right back in New Jersey. I was born and raised here, went to college here, married two Jersey girls, raised my family here. I work here, too, for the *Star Ledger*, the state's biggest and best newspaper.

So far I've lived in fifteen towns and six counties in New Jersey, from the family homestead in Spring Lake (born) to the parkside Normandy Tudor in Summit (raised), to a boarding house in Woodbury and an apartment in West Deptford (navy days), to a dorm room in New Brunswick (college), to a first-married apartment in Bloomfield, to a first-home wreck of a handyman's special in Morris Township, to a coop efficiency in East Orange (after the wreck of the first marriage), to a co-owned minimanse Victorian in Maplewood (with two fireplaces in the living room), to a couple of rooming houses in Madison and Chatham Township, to an apartment in Denville and another one in Boonton, to a rented house with my new wife in Boonton Township, to a cozy postwar Cape in Boonton (our first home), to a cozy postwar Cape in Mountain Lakes, and, maybe, finally, mercifully, to the 1949 split-level which is walking distance from all schools and big enough to accommodate all the kids.

And that's just my personal life.

My professional life moved me around the state, too. I started in the newspaper business right out of the service as a seventeen-dollar-a-night stringer, then a ninety-dollar-a-week part-time sportswriter, for the *Daily Record* of Morristown, spending most evenings and Saturday nights in either town council chambers or high school gyms throughout Morris and Sussex Counties. Then I did two years in the Jersey Rust Belt as an editor at the (now-dead) *News Tribune*. (Does anybody else miss that paper's art deco cartoon newsboy, which overlooked the Woodbridge

Turnpike interchange?) After a five-year stint as a nearly well-known sports columnist in New York, I returned to Jersey, to the *Star-Ledger*, the paper I'd grown up with.

For the most part, my early job at the *Ledger* was to go out and write about things that were interesting. Simple enough. I not only knew the state from my many moves, but had toured it as a kid with my father, a teacher with great geographical, historical, and social curiosity and the restlessness to explore it.

My father was born in 1923, a member of the Great American Middle Class that would elevate car culture in America. His generation was the first to truly experience the wholesale freedom of the automobile—the first to enjoy the automobile's mass-production affordability and emerging reliability and the burgeoning network of good roads.

They could, anytime they wanted, "go for a ride." They could explore. They could drive beyond the cities and transportation hubs, deep into the countryside, and find quiet, hidden places. After World War II, these people moved away from cities simply because they knew they could.

During the war, my father traveled extensively through Europe, the Mideast, South America and the South Pacific, and visited nearly every port in the United States. He had lived in Italy part-time as a boy and in Mexico as a G.I. Bill student, so he was fluent in English and Italian and conversant in Spanish and French. He wanted to be a language teacher, but in the full rut of the baby boom he found it easier to get work as an elementary school teacher.

With his growing family, he became a weekend wanderer in the 1950s, 1960s, and 1970s, and I discovered much of New Jersey while leaning up against the front bench seat of whatever station wagon we had, looking over his shoulder, watching the road go by, learning. He seemed to know a little bit about everything, everywhere—the Shore, the Pine Barrens, the cities, the mountains, and the farmlands. We climbed the Statue of Liberty, the High Point Monument, and the lighthouses at Barnegat and Cape May. We discovered the deserted villages at Allaire and Batsto, swam at Hopatcong and Spruce Run, walked the streets of country towns like Clinton, Flemington, and Lambertville. We saw the grand mansions of Short Hills and Cape May, witnessed the elegant decay of High Street in Newark and the downtowns that became ghost towns in Asbury Park, Paterson, and Plainfield. We saw where Thomas A. Edison, Albert Einstein, and Walt Whitman worked, where George Washington's legend was made, where Alexander Hamilton's illustrious life ended. We heard the thunder of the Great Falls and the rush of wind through the dune grass at Island Beach in dead winter. We saw hawks circling and deer bolting.

I got my driver's license in 1974 and quickly found I had inherited my father's restlessness. First in his Chevelle, then in my Honda Civic, I explored the backroads, covering great distances, plumbing the depths of the state. I climbed the winding ridges in the Highlands, kicked up dirt on the sandy roads of the Pinelands, found the roads that dead-ended down at the Delaware River or through the grasslands to the Delaware Bay, traversed the Great Swamp with lights out in the dark, trespassed on the private roads of the Somerset Hills, felt the car shudder on Ocean Avenue during winter nor'easters.

The goal was always the same: to travel unobstructed. To escape the suburbs, their downtowns and their traffic lights and their school zones and their local cops and their station wagons doing thirty-five in a forty. To find the flat country roads or those that wound and climbed and dropped through the hills of the countryside. To find the roads that made you want a two-seat British roadster or a full-dresser Harley.

To get lost—and lost in daydreams. To be the stranger in the diner, the traveling loner.

To be alone together with someone happy to be there, to talk and tell everything, or to ride in silence in her company, her head on your shoulder. To find the private hillside or curve by the river, to be the one who found those places, to be the one who made those memories.

To see great estates with their mansions hidden by mature trees at the end of long driveways and wonder, Who lives there? and dream about possibilities and futures. To see abandoned farms with their sagging Victorian houses and collapsed barns, and worry about how broken life could become.

To see animals: thoroughbreds and draft horses, the regal llamas and common sheep, the dignified but doomed Black Angus, and the dumb, prehistoric-looking Jersey milkers.

These rides, always endless, always too short, helped me discover lots of things—about myself, about girls, and about our compact little state. I learned New Jersey was a place of enormous geologic, geographic, and cultural scope, a place worthy of scientific and social study, a place where a writer could work.

The great outcrops of rock in the north and the flatlands of the south tell the story of prehistoric New Jersey, an abridged version of Earth history. Likewise, human history in New Jersey is a microcosm of American history.

Let's start at the beginning.

The Precambrian granite and crystalline rock formations of the Highlands are among the earliest on Earth, dating back four and a half billion years. The formation of the Kittatinny Ridge and Valley in the extreme northwest corner of the state began in the Paleozoic Era, about 570 million years ago, when ocean life first appeared, and continued until the final folding of the Appalachians in the Permian Period, when insects and reptiles roamed the earth.

The sedimentary rock of the Piedmont, the area between the Highlands and the Coastal Plains, was formed during the Triassic and Jurassic Periods of the Mesozoic Era, beginning 225 million years ago when birds and early dinosaurs made their entrance. The Inner Coastal Plain, stretching from the Raritan Bay down to Gloucester County at a forty-five degree angle, was formed during the Cretaceous Period, when dinosaur life reached full bloom. Finally, the Outer Coastal Plain formed mostly in the Tertiary Period of the Cenozoic Era, beginning sixty-five million years ago, as primitive mammals developed. Some of the fringes of the Outer Coastal Plain developed during the relatively recent Quaternary Period, the time during which humankind evolved and came to dominate the earth.

And this is why you find unique, hard fluorescent minerals in Franklin, utilitarian traprock in the quarries of the Watchungs, and the permeable, loose sedimentary rock in the water-rich Pinelands.

And this is why New Jersey's surface geography—from the dizzying cliffs of the Palisades to the blunted peaks of the Highlands and Kittatinny Ridges, to the rolling swells of the Morris, Hunterdon, and Somerset Hills, to the soil-wealthy agricultural belts through Monmouth and the deep south counties, to the flat, sandy beaches of the 127-mile "Jersey Shore" beginning at Sandy Hook and ending at Cape May, to the still-desolate marshlands of the Delaware Bay—is a landscape artist's dream.

These drastic natural differences, along with natural resources that shaped industry, have fed cultural diversity, too. Diversity was a buzzword in Clinton-era America, trumpeting the nation's growing racial, religious, and ethnic mix. The U.S. Census 2000 data on New Jersey shows as many Hispanics as African Americans, and a triple-digit rise for Asians—especially in parts of Bergen and Middlesex counties.

But the state has always been ethnically and culturally diverse: When the first federal census was taken in 1790, New Jerseyans of English descent were only 47 percent of the population. Sixteen percent were Dutch, 9 percent German, 8 percent Scots, and 8 percent African American. Only Pennsylvania, among the thirteen colonies, had people with more diverse backgrounds. (By today's standards, this is hardly a beautiful mosaic, but that doesn't mean all was well in colonial America: Dutch and Swedish settlers battled for control of South Jersey in the early 1600s, Presbyterians and Episcopalians burned each other's churches down during the American Revolution, and the ethnic clustering that later would be associated with blue-collar neighborhoods in industrial cities first took hold in the early American farmlands.)

Likewise, New Jersey's early cultural diversity among white people was a byproduct of the landscape. The whalers, fishers, and other seagoers of the Shore region, the miners of the Highlands, the dairy farmers of rock-strewn Warren and Sussex, the vegetable growers of Central and South Jersey, the muskrat trappers and oyster gatherers of the Delaware

Bay, all created cultures inherent to their regions. The later cultural diversity driven by new immigrant groups only added to the mix.

All of this—the dramatic differences in landscape, the regional differences of the people—is the New Jersey I know.

It is a state of infinite natural beauty, a state of intricate human patterns. A state where you can see a lot in a little time. This is, so simply put, the overriding theme of this book. New Jersey is a restless state for restless people. A state for wanderers to explore.

There is no shortage of ways to get around New Jersey by car.

Two Interstates (78 and 80) begin their cross-country treks here, linking the New York area with points west. The New Jersey Turnpike is the overland route between New York and Philadelphia, a modern road that has superseded many historic routes. The Garden State Parkway runs the state north to south, delivering the tourism economy to the Shore.

The circuitous Interstate 287 loops the metropolitan area, connecting the Highlands to Somerset Hills to the Middlesex chemical belt. Interstate 195 beelines from Trenton to the Shore, like a belt at the state's waist. The Atlantic City Expressway can move you from the Philadelphia suburbs to gameland in just about an hour.

Then there are the U.S. highways—1, 9, 22, 30, 46, 130, 202, and 206—and 2,267 miles of state highways marked by their circular shields.

All these make up the state's primary network of roads.

But they won't take you into every corner of the state, to out-of-the-way places like Plumbsock or Myrtle Grove in Sussex County, or Cedarville and Dividing Creek in Cumberland, or Rosemont in lower Hunterdon, or Pipers Corner in the heart of the Pinelands.

They won't take you deep into the Stokes, Wharton, or Belleplain state forests. They won't take you along the waters of the old Delaware and Raritan Canal in Griggstown, or the trout-rich white waters of the South Branch of the Raritan, or the deep mountain lakes of the Kittatinny chain. They won't take you over one of the earliest roads on the continent, the Old Mine Road in Sussex County, or to Sergeantsville, the home of the state's last covered bridge.

They won't take you to the place where George Washington wrote his farewell orders at Rocky Hill, or to the tavern at Centerton where Lafayette may have helped plot Revolutionary strategy, or to the town of Swartswood, where a British colonial officer named Anthony Swartwout and most of his family were massacred by Indians.

To truly explore New Jersey, you have to take the secondary roads. Backroads, New Jersey.

The secondary roads—also known as the intercounty roads or "500" series—are a 6,788-mile network of mostly two-lane highways. These roads, marked by blue-and-yellow five-sided shields bearing county names, make up over 20 percent of New Jersey's 33,741 miles of public roads.

The odd-numbered "500" roads run north-south, the evens east-west.

Route 501—the first secondary—runs from the upper northeast corner of the state at Rockleigh in Bergen County, down along the Hudson River through Hoboken and Jersey City, to its end at the Bayonne Bridge. Route 502, the first east-west road, goes from Alpine, overlooking the Hudson, and heads uphill to Oakland some twenty miles away.

The highest-numbered secondary road is 585, which skirts Absecon and Lukes bays in Atlantic County, then reappears as a four-mile spur connecting Burleigh to State Highway 47 halfway down the Cape May peninsula.

The longest—and perhaps most beautiful—is Route 519, which clocks in at about eighty- seven miles from Stockton in lower Hunterdon County to Mount Salem in Sussex, just south of High Point. The next longest, at eighty-four miles, is 527, which runs from Singac at the Essex–Passaic County border to just outside Toms River in Ocean County.

The "500" roads were set up as a network by the state legislature just before the passage of the federal Interstate Highway Act of 1956. The purpose was to set up a secondary road network to complement the state highway system, which was formed in 1912, and to make the intercounty roads eligible for federal funds.

What the secondary road system provides is a well-maintained network of "backroads." The "500" roads are good roads—smoothly paved and clearly marked as they wind through the countryside, connecting New Jersey's small towns and main streets.

These roads give you a chance to see New Jersey's geologic diversity firsthand. The sixty-three-mile drive from Hightstown to Tuckerton on Route 539 begins in the soil-rich open farmlands of Central Jersey. Before long, the soil turns sandy and the stubby pines crop up as the road cuts south through the Pinelands. Soon enough, the pines all but disappear, the sandy soil becomes all sand, and the road ends on the coast.

The fifty-four-mile drive on Route 553 gives a similar view of changing geography and its effect on local economies. Down in Port Norris, on the Maurice River a mile from the Delaware Bay, the road goes past the remnants of New Jersey's oystering industry, the hamlets of Bivalve and Shellpile. This is an area of meandering streams traveling to the bay over marshy lowlands, where the only thing that grows is swamp grass. Farther up 553 into Cumberland, Salem, and Gloucester counties, the road cuts through one of the richest agricultural areas on the East Coast. The highly mechanized industrial farms there produce millions of bushels of produce a year, and it is not unusual to see migrant workers harvesting crops on smaller farms.

These "500" roads are where you meet New Jersey history.

Many of the secondary roads have their roots in colonial times and some go back to Native Americans. Route 511, which begins near Morristown and ends at Greenwood Lake, follows a trail used by the Munsee (a subtribe of the Lenape Indians) through the Highlands. The trail area, which followed the Wanaque River valley out of Greenwood Lake down into the Pompton region, was a fertile hunting and fishing corridor. Colonial Americans found it useful, too. The water power of the mountain rivers and the abundance of iron ore in the earth made it ideal for a string of foundries. The old Indian trail became a much-traveled colonial road, connecting the Morristown area with the ironworks at Hanover,

Boonton, and Ringwood, and serving as a supply line for the Continental army.

These roads are where you understand New Jersey sociology.

Route 510 in Newark begins its thirty-one-mile crawl west as Market Street in downtown Newark and tells the story of population migration in twentieth-century New Jersey. The road captures much of what is New Jersey today: the energy of the city and the placidity of the country, urban decay and suburban sprawl, urban renewal and rural decay, the undeniable segregation of races, the death of manufacturing and the rise of the service economy, the historical and ever-present shift of affluence west.

These roads are never the fastest or most direct way to get anywhere. They meander. They go through residential areas and school zones. They bog down as they become Main Street in many towns. But when you break out of the towns and hit the country, they are a pleasure to drive.

Let the people in a hurry take the Interstates, let the shoppers and errand runners take the state highways. Leave the secondary roads to the explorers, and the restless, and the wanderers. And therein lies the true beauty of the secondary roads—so much to see, and so few to see it.

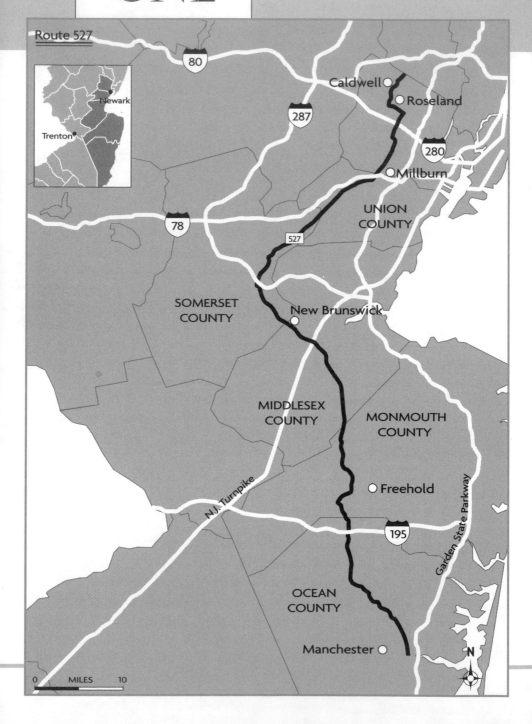

CHAPTER
ONE

Route 527

Newark
Trenton

80

287

Caldwell
Roseland

280

Millburn

78

UNION
COUNTY

527

SOMERSET
COUNTY

New Brunswick

MIDDLESEX
COUNTY

MONMOUTH
COUNTY

Freehold

N.J. Turnpike

195

Garden State Parkway

OCEAN
COUNTY

Manchester

N

0   MILES   10

Route 527 is an interior road, an eighty-four-mile curved spine of a road that mimics New Jersey's coastline. It is a road of great geographic, economic, and social contrast, not the quickest way to get anywhere, but a road that gives away many of the state's secrets.

At the top end, 527 goes along the ridges of the Watchungs, and it is a continual and winding asphalt overlook of mountains in the distant west and the towns in the valleys in between. It runs here through some of the state's best traditional old-English affluent suburbs, the Tudored and Colonialed Caldwells, Essex Fells, and Short Hills. This is the New Jersey of country clubs and country day schools, of "convenience to the city." This is the New Jersey of cultural and civic societies, of serving on boards and committees and councils of towns and churches and art institutions. Life is more than good in this New Jersey. It is privileged.

In the middle, 527 runs through industrial New Jersey, over the Raritan and its abandoned ferry and ghost boats, the empty factories and the small businesses staggering under the weight of a collapsed economy. This is the New Jersey of weathered Cape Cods, the meager dream homes of a generation of Central Jersey chemical workers from the Amboys who moved to the suburbs of Old Bridge. This is the New Jersey of one-person trucking and excavation businesses, of hot rods for sale on the front yards of battered houses, of greasers and bikers and go-go bars. This is the Jersey of Springsteen, away from the boardwalk.

At the bottom, 527 runs through the sandy flatlands of rural western Monmouth and Ocean counties, into the northeastern edge of the Pines. This is the New Jersey of junk dealers outside Englishtown, of stand-alone evangelical churches, of Confederate flags in windows, of sagging barns and broken chicken coops, of sad-eyed mutts and tired, bored horses, of a country remoteness and rural poverty not often associated with the nation's most densely populated and wealthiest state. This is

1. Junk shops outside Englishtown on Route 527.
Photo by Mark Di Ionno.

the New Jersey where you can get lost in the woods, and fear being found
by anyone but police.

How does so much fit on one road?

Aside from 527's nearly hundred-mile length, the road does a
connect-the-dots meander through parts of about a dozen downtowns. It
cuts over or under four Interstates (280, 78, 287, 195) and the Turnpike
and runs alongside long stretches of U.S. Routes 22 and 9. It also intersects more than a dozen heavily trafficked state highways. In this sense,
calling it a spine is literal, although it would be among the last routes a
time-conscious driver would pick to drive north to south. In midday,
with sunny conditions, it is about a three-hour drive, end to end. All the
east-to-west intersections make parts of 527 a heavily trafficked road, as
do a number of enormous employers—St. Barnabas Medical Center in
Livingston, Prudential in Roseland, Johnson and Johnson in New
Brunswick, to name a few.

But the slow-go of 527 gives you a chance to soak in all that Jersey
diversity. The road starts as Mountain Avenue in North Caldwell, climb-

ing off Route 23 up the Watchungs, putting a panoramic view of the Little Falls/Totowa area in your rearview mirror. (Fans of the TV show *The Sopranos* will recognize the part of the road that tunnels through mountain rock, shown each week in the Jersey montage during the opening theme.) Roadside in North Caldwell is a mix of old and new affluence— big houses from the turn of the century in the Tudor, Colonial, and Craftsman modes, and big stone Italianate and Norman houses from the building booms of the 1880s and 1890s.

Downtown Caldwell, nestled in a Watchung valley, is a prototypical suburban Essex downtown—family-owned businesses, an in-town gas station, no shortage of delis and small restaurants, a big Presbyterian church in the center, and a Catholic church just outside the business district. Caldwell has something no other place has—the birthplace of

2. Route 527 as it cuts through the Watchung Mountains in North Caldwell. Photo by Mark Di Ionno.

Grover Cleveland, the only president born in New Jersey and the only one to get elected, unelected, then elected again. In the year he was defeated, he actually won the popular vote, but lost the electoral vote. Cleveland was also the first president to marry in the White House, and the nation watched as his young family grew. Cleveland's father was pastor of the First Presbyterian Church in town, and the current building is the centerpiece of the downtown. The town is named after a Presbyterian hero, Rev. James Caldwell—"The Fighting Parson"—who used his pulpit to further the cause of the American Revolution nearby in what is now Union County.

Route 527 is Bloomfield Avenue—the commercial main drag of Essex—for a few blocks in Caldwell, before it hooks south at the Presbyterian church. Here 527 becomes Roseland Avenue and goes through Essex Fells.

Essex Fells, like the Short Hills section of Millburn and Llewellyn Park in West Orange, is a planned executive community. Essex Fells was the dream of banker Anthony Drexel, of the Philadelphia Drexels. The land was purchased in 1888 by his son-in-law John R. Fell (the first of the Essex Fells). By 1902, the little town was incorporated as a borough, and it remains today the smallest town in Essex County, with about twenty-two hundred residents living in about one and one-third square miles. Through careful planning and strict zoning, Essex Fells has maintained its exclusivity. Even the houses along the busiest street, 527, are mansion-sized with parklike lots. There are no commercial properties in Essex Fells. It's strictly residential. And for students of residential architecture, Essex Fells is a case study in Better Suburbs, Late Victorian Era and Early Twentieth Century. Its houses are Tudor, Norman, Dutch Colonial, Colonial Revival, and an array of Victorians—Stick, Queen Anne, and Shingle. Substantial homes of brick, clapboard, shingle, or stucco.

Neighboring Roseland is a case study in Suburban Sprawl, Late Twentieth Century. On the expansive property of the former Becker dairy farm is an approximately two-million-square-foot region of office space, much of it occupied by Prudential. Around the office parks are some townhome complexes. All sit on a mountain slope just north of Interstate 280, easy on, easy off for commuters. The office buildings are plain and angular—squat concrete-and-glass blots on the westward-looking vista. The townhomes are equally plain. In all, these buildings are nondescript 1980s architecture, no better or worse than thousands just like them, the architecture of sameness, the architecture of zoning-board–proof, high-density ratables. The footprint of Roseland's agricultural past can be seen in spots. There are a few old farmhouses still on the main road, and the town historical society has exhibits on eighteenth century farming.

Through Roseland and Livingston and into Short Hills, 527 runs a ridge on the long western slope of Second Watchung Mountain. It overlooks the Passaic River valley and in the distance are the next series of rises—Foremost Mountain in Montville, Sheep Hill in Boonton, the Tourne Mountain right behind it, and Watnong Mountain in Parsippany, which is topped by luxury condos that look like concrete bunkers defending the valley. Besides the concrete bunkers, there are other landmarks, like the steeple of the Boonton Presbyterian Church and the bell towers at St. Elizabeth's College in Convent Station.

It is an impressive view. While the eastern face of the Watchungs give a more dramatic view of the Manhattan skyline, the Newark Basin, and the bridges that connect them, the western view is subtler. It is a view of green hills that turn purple at sunset and form a black outline on the silvery or deep blue night sky.

In summer the tree cover dominates the landscape with different shades and depths of greens and blues. In early morning and early evening, the air is heavy, thick with humidity from all those trees. When the sun streaks through gathering or scattering clouds, that trapped heavy air makes the late afternoon sky look like something from the brushstrokes of Michelangelo.

In fall, the greens are replaced by the autumnal browns and reds and yellows, and the hills turn golden at sunrise and sunset. The air clears, and, up from and away from the megalopolis groundlight, the stars stand out a little clearer. Then there are the moving stars: the headlights of the endless procession of air traffic, sailing through darkness, silent on the meridian, ready to angle down for Newark or La Guardia.

Winter grays the hills, and brings out even clearer night lights, and spring renews the cycle.

It gets harder to appreciate the Watchungs as 527 cuts through Livingston, where tightly packed suburban neighborhoods and strip malls make paying attention to the road a priority. Past St. Barnabas, the road crosses into the Short Hills section of Millburn. The far northern part of Old Short Hills Road, which 527 is called here, has homes built in the 1960s and 1970s. Deeper into the section you get the mansions and high-end executive homes that Stewart Hartshorn envisioned when he bought 1,552 acres over seven hills in 1877, on which to build an estate enclave. Truth is, the Short Hills section of Millburn is part rich, old suburb and part suburban sprawl. The old parts on the winding roads north of Hobart Avenue and south of Hartshorn Drive have that distinctive gas-lit suburban Essex feel. Outside of those borders, the executive ranch and split level become more common. So does the cul-de-sac.

Downtown Millburn today reflects the wealth of the Short Hills area. The stores are specialty shops, true boutiques. Millburn Avenue, as 527 is called here, has changed quite a bit from when I worked for Uncle Cookie (real name, Rocco Sammartino), who owned Koll's luncheonette next to the Millburn movie theater in a storefront that today is a jewelry store.

Cook was a squat guy in a white apron and white short-sleeved shirt. He wore thick-soled shoes because he was on his feet fourteen hours a day, and he usually had a cigar clenched between his teeth.

"Hey, Cook, give me an egg salad on white, easy on the ashes," customers would say.

It was a small universe, this little luncheonette run by my father's best friend, inhabited by town workers, shopkeepers, and clerks, regulars all. Cook and his brother, Sal, who worked the register, and most of the customers were Millburn old-timers—working-class townies who operated in a hemisphere unknown and invisible to the transient New York executives who lived in Short Hills.

In this world, I was "Tony's kid," a generational extension of their old neighborhood. In this world, I was no longer a kid, but a working kid— old enough to learn the language of men, blue-collar men talking blue streaks, talking mean streaks. Behind the counter in a white apron, making coffees and sandwiches, I was accepted into that company. This was not the language of women and girls, or the language of the Short Hills stockbroker set. This was the secret language of backstreet Millburn. Every Saturday after work, my father would come to get me and hang around while I cleaned up. I saw him in those minutes not as my dad but as one of the boys. I saw him step out of the role of suburban father into something more comfortable, something closer to who he really was. Maybe he saw me the same way, I don't know. All I know is something happened in that store that couldn't have happened in our normal family setting, and as downtowns like Millburn go upscale, I hope there's still someplace where some kid gets to feel the same thing.

The road gets confusing out of Millburn. It turns into Morris Avenue (Route 124) where Millburn, Springfield, and Summit come together. The building of Interstate 78 changed the course of 527, and it only goes one way—toward Millburn—out of Summit. But you can pick it up again in Summit by driving down Route 124, going to Broad Street, and hooking over Middle Avenue to Morris Avenue. The road here goes past Bryant Park and through East Summit (see chapter 8) and climbs Second Watchung Mountain. At the steepest part, just below Overlook Hospital, 527 makes a sharp left turn toward Mountainside. Here it becomes Glenside Avenue and runs parallel with Interstate 78 through Watchung Reservation.

It wasn't always that way. The Interstate was a long time coming.

Announced by the federal government in 1957, it was to be a parallel east-west companion to Interstate 80, which cut through the northern part of the state. Interstate 78 would connect the lower end of the metro region at Newark to points west. The highway stalled at the Watchung Reservation for close to two decades, as local officials and environmentalists fought the federal government over the plan. When 78 was finally completed in 1986, it cut through the northernmost part of the reservation on a mountain ridge. Wildlife bridges were built to allow animals to cross from the large part of the two-thousand-acre reservation to the six-acre sliver across the road.

Of all the changes and development I've seen in New Jersey, the one that leaves me most wistful is the Route 78 link through the Watchung Reservation.

When I was boy, we could walk from our home to the steep wooded pit of the mountain we called "Elephant's Grave," cross 527 (Glenside Avenue), and spend full days exploring the reservation.

The days in the reservation were endless. We went in while the grass was still dewy, carrying canvas backpacks with food and water, maybe a jacket, a flashlight, and a first aid kit. We'd hike, get lost, end up in a residential neighborhood in Mountainside or Berkeley Heights, go back into the woods, get lost again, luck onto familiar paths, then emerge late in the afternoon, sweaty and bug-bit, tired and dragging ourselves back across 527, up "Elephant's Grave," relieved to find civilization again before dinner.

There was much to explore. The Watchung Reservation had a stable, two lakes, a deserted Nike missile base, a deserted village, an abandoned quarry with small cliffs to scale, and a ninety-foot mountaintop water tower to climb with an observation deck that put you on top of the world. On Surprise Lake there was a place to rent rowboats with a snack bar and nature museum with Indian artifacts, stuffed birds, and critters and animal fetuses in formaldehyde.

The highway didn't change all that. The Trailside Nature Museum is still there, but it's more antiseptic. The stable has moved from 527 and been rebuilt over the Nike base. The deserted village is still there, right off 527, in some stage of restoration. The water tower is still there, but the observation deck was torn off when the words "insurance liability" became part of our everyday vocabulary. And the small cliffs of the old quarry remain, posted with warning signs that maybe were there when I was a kid, but I didn't notice. The highway changed the natural stream flow to Surprise Lake, which today is choked by lilypads and weeds. The lake died, taking the rowboat and snack bar concession with it.

When I was a young teen, tripping headfirst out of boyhood, my first girlfriend lived at the bottom of "Elephant's Grave" in a house on Glenside Avenue separated by the woods from the rest of town. This had good and bad points. The good points were the assured privacy of the trees and brush, the stillness of the dusk cover; the bad points were that I had to run back through the dark woods after our nervous explorations in the disappearing light.

I can still hear the crickets and screech owls from those humid summer nights when the smell of honeysuckle mixed with the overwhelming fresh scent of a teenage girl. I remember her clear, blue eyes and how she peeked when we kissed. I remember how she hung her arms around my neck and how I tilted my head to meet hers and how it made me feel taller and more protective than I really was. (Now a middle-aged man with a beautiful teenage daughter, I am nostalgic and jealous and wary, reminded of that lost youth and innocence.)

Her name was Ellen and she lived on 527 and I loved her as much as a fifteen-year-old can.

Route 78 didn't change that. Time did. All the highway did was erase some of the evidence. Our mountain path is gone now, and so is Ellen's house, its foundation buried under tons of crushed rock and asphalt, unknown to the thousands of people who drive over it everyday at the speed of life.

Earlier boyhood, of course, held different sensory excitements.

The climb up the circular stairs of the water tower. This was a dizzying lift-off above the tree line, an ascent into a view of the Raritan Basin that proved the world was big out there and there was life beyond our little town, waiting for us to discover it.

The spooky emptiness of the Nike missile base, a Cold War white elephant, built in 1955 as part of a nationwide strategic air defense system and abandoned less than ten years later. The Watchung Reservation base, I would learn later, was one in a string designed to protect the metro area. Others were built on Sandy Hook and in East Hanover, Wayne, Mahwah, and Middletown. The early AJAX missiles had only a twenty-five mile range (so that the enemy planes they were designed to knock down would presumably crash with their nuclear bombs in the middle of suburbia), but missile technology quickly improved, and the next-generation Hercules missiles had a range of ninety miles, traveled at twenty-six hundred miles per hour, and were themselves capable of carrying nuclear warheads. Within a few years, long-range missile technology made local bases obsolete, and the Watchung Reservation base was closed in 1963.

I knew none of this as a boy. I just knew the deserted buildings and barracks were a bizarre ghost town in the middle of the woods and the park police would run you out if they caught you back there. I also heard there was a secret underground bunker, but never figured out how to get down there. (This, in fact, was true. The missiles were stacked underground, to be moved by elevator to the launch pads.) I also knew the abandoned towers on top of the mountain (where Governor Livingston High School is today) were somehow connected to the missile base (they were, in fact, its radar station). I also knew it could be a dangerous place—I knew a kid who fell about forty feet off one of the towers and broke both his legs.

The deserted village, I would learn later, was a place called Feltville. Its founder, David Felt, opened paper mills and built a company town on 760 acres in the valley between First and Second Watchung Mountains. By 1852, seven years after Felt bought the land, his 'ville had two hundred residents who lived in thirteen double houses and two dormitories and worshiped in an Episcopal church that doubled as the company store. Felt retired in 1860 and the village was sold to a sarsaparilla maker who went belly up. By 1875, Feltville was deserted. Nearly a century later, the people were ghosts, and what was left of their village a dilapidated collection of sagging frame houses sitting mysteriously in the middle of the woods, waiting for preteen boys to skulk around and get spooked.

The crumbling traprock cliffs in the reservation and the woods around them were perfect for boy games like manhunt (which is basically team hide-and-go-seek).

The rocks were just dangerous enough. They climbed like narrow stairs, giving you plenty of footing, and there was plenty of well-rooted brush to grab hold of. But there were enough loose rocks to make you slip now and then or to send a small avalanche of bricks below.

These rocks were high enough to be exciting but not enough to kill you in a fall—unless, of course, you landed wrong. The best cliffs were over by Seeley's Pond, right off 527. We spent a lot of time down there, a pack of young naturalists who worried only about bee stings, poison ivy, falling off the old dam with its trickle of waterfall, or tumbling down a cliff. Most of us were Boy Scouts, and knew we were as capable of heroic action as the kids in the back of *Boy's Life* magazine—those kids immortalized in comic strip form for doing things like saving the little brother who fell through the ice or rescuing the next-door neighbor's unattended kids from a house fire. We knew we could splint a broken leg if a kid fell off a cliff, or suck the poison out of their leg if he got bit by a killer snake, or give him mouth-to-mouth if he went under in Seeley's Pond. But, except for poison ivy and a few scraped knees, nothing bad ever happened.

I remember how sad I was, then, a few years later, when I read about a teenaged kid who drowned in Seeley's Pond after a bunch of other kids threw him in and then threw rocks at him so he couldn't get out. He tried to swim to the other side and didn't make it.

I was saddened by the cruelty of it, by the indifference to life. I was saddened by the unheard calls for help from the kid who died. It was evidence to me that boyhood had changed.

No one is out there dusting for fossils or climbing rocks or identifying trees. No one is out there thinking about running for help or diving into the pond with a rope or trapping air in a shirt to make a flotation device. There is no one out there who reads *Boy's Life*. Suburban childhood is different now. Kids no longer wander and discover their surroundings with a makeshift group of available friends. Instead, they see the world not from their bicycle but from the back of a minivan . . . not as part of an unstructured group but as part of a traveling team. The leader is the best athlete, not the kid who knows the right path to get everyone home. Lost is the sense of adventure, replaced by a timetable of weekend games and events, a chauffeuring schedule kept by moms and dads.

3. Development in Warren Township.
Photo by Mark Di Ionno.

You can't blame Route 78 for that, either.

West of the Watchung Reservation, 527 runs through the valley of the first and second Watchung Ridges. This was pretty much a link to the country before the highway was completed. But the highway has brought things like the Villas on the Park in Berkeley Heights and the Windmere development in Warren Township, in which the rooflines of the clustered single-family houses form an artificial ridge against the backdrop of the real mountain line.

Sadly, Warren Township officials must have never met a blueprint they didn't like. The town has been overbuilt—and badly—along 527, which is Washington Valley Road through here. There are strip malls, McMansion developments, and stand-alone banks, all right on top of each other, shoehorned into lots on the hillside, with hardly any greenways. The drive through here is frustrating at best and treacherous at worst, a game of SUV and minivan bumper cars.

And then something beautiful happens—527 takes a turn up Morning Glory Road, and it brings you back to the presprawl Watchungs, the

Watchungs of fresh mountain air, of German health retreats, hidden lake communities, summer camps, and nudist colonies. The Watchungs that were remote, even a little wild—a place to get away from it all. A place where some of the local mountain folk were so culturally distant from the big city, they might as well have been in a West Virginia hollow.

Up Morning Glory Road is a series of small houses, shacks really, and old hunting lodges. "Rabbits all sizes for sale," says one sign. The requisite junked cars and tractors litter the yards, and spare parts for the running models lie in the driveways. You know this little slice of hillbilly New Jersey won't last too far into the new millennium before the bulldozers come. As you climb the road, the houses become larger, some monumental and modern, perched on the mountain ridge with a drop-dead view of the Raritan Basin.

The Watchungs, as mountains go, are among the smallest on the East Coast, nowhere near the size of the mid-range Appalachians. But the crest of Morning Glory Road is among the highest points of the blunt range, and the view comes up suddenly on the winding road. It is surprisingly high, a south- and eastward look from an altitude for a low-flying plane. Unlike the earlier 527 views—which look over sloping valleys and mountain vistas—this view is of the flat and long New Jersey interior coastal plain. (For a great view that does not include oncoming traffic and roadside mailboxes, visit Washington Rock State Park not too far from 527.) The road descends the mountain toward Route 22, at an angle resembling a small plane approach. When 527 touches down near Route 22, you seem to be in a different part of the country.

North of Route 22, 527 runs through some of the finest suburbs New Jersey has to offer (save the small hillbilly enclave of Morning Glory Road).

South of Route 22, it visits a different New Jersey. The road crosses into Bound Brook and becomes flat as the landscape. On either side are Cape Cods on lots thirty-five feet wide, one after another, with town recycling buckets at the curb. The road heads downtown, flood-ravaged by Hurricane Floyd in 1999 and still staggering back. Downtown Bound Brook is an eclectic mix of antique shops and galleries (because of the low rents), mom-and-pop restaurants, bodegas with signs in Spanish, and go-go bars with names like Torpedoes, Private Dancers, Showplace, and Ooh-La-La. The people are an eclectic mix of dark-clad artsy sophisticates, Hispanic day laborers, and bikers from Central Jersey.

The road turns at the sandstone Pillar of Fire building, the forerunner of the fundamentalist Zarephath religious enclave in Franklin Township, goes along the Raritan River, and becomes Main Street in South Bound Brook and Easton Avenue in Franklin. A stretch of 527 there gives a two-hundred-year snapshot of American sociology in two driving seconds. It's where you find the home of Hendrick Fisher, an archpatriot of the American Revolution and archenemy of the British. General William Howe wanted him hanged on sight and the British raided and ransacked his home in 1777. Fisher died in 1779 at age eighty-two and is buried in the family plot on the property, which is today owned by the Ukrainian Orthodox Church. That Fisher was a freedom fighter is understandably important to the Ukrainian-Americans, who fought the Soviet empire, and they take great pride in owning and maintaining the home in all its colonial glory (see color plate 1).

Route 527 now runs alongside the Raritan into New Brunswick, where the historic district was plowed under by the downtown revitalization of the 1990s. Back when I was at Rutgers in 1979–1980, the downtown was seedy and a little dangerous. Now, with the new Johnson & Johnson headquarters and the growing hospital empires, it has become antiseptic. Fern bars have replaced the go-go joints and bean sprout restaurants have replaced the grease pits, but, hey, that's progress. Why fight it?

From New Brunswick, 527 takes a turn for the worse. It is Route 18— a bumpy, congested, hateful mess of a road for a while—then cuts out again, becoming what amounts to a Route 18 service road through the South River area. Here you see the dregs of Central Jersey—a capped landfill, an abandoned ferryboat rotting in the Raritan, used car lots, warehouses of corrugated metal, and confusing roads signs. Finding 527 through this maze is a challenge, but once you know it becomes Old Bridge-Englishtown Road, it's easier to figure out.

Unlike the northern part of 527 through the Watchungs, the road here couldn't be flatter or straighter. Central Jersey ticks by in mile-tenths . . . the diners . . . the small strips anchored by convenience stores . . . the Levittown-like neighborhoods of capes and small, lookalike ranches . . . the trucking places . . . the gravel places. . . .

And suddenly the Jersey rust belt fades into something else. The signs change. Up come the "Canary Bird Farm" and "Farm Fresh Brown Eggs, $1.50 a dozen." Yards become cluttered with yard-sale junk designed to attract the flea market crowd heading toward Englishtown. English-town itself is a strange mix of classy looking antique shops, historic buildings like the Village Inn and Tennent Church (both visited by Washington during the Battle of Monmouth), and the sprawling, ragged stands of the flea market. This is where suburban/country affluence rubs up against plain old country.

South of Englishtown is an Agway, a neighborhood of rundown, four-walled block houses, and a development called Manalapan Hills, with homes selling for a quarter-million dollars.

The Battlefield Collection at Pine Valley in Freehold Township con-sists of new minimanses with square-footage equal to the pretensions of the name. Around the corner is a battered livestock farm, with sagging weathered barn and a rusted pickup, no lie, on cinder blocks.

It stays like this all the way through Ocean County. You can hardly believe the road that took you through Short Hills, Essex Fells, and the grand mansions of high-end suburbia is now taking you past the one-room little red Faith Bible Church, near the tidy Southwood Mobile Home Village (see color plate 2). You can hardly believe, as you drive past the scrub pines rooted in their sandy-soiled flatness, that less than two hours ago you were driving through a hardwood mountain forest. It's an eighty-four-mile drive, a backroad through layers of social strata and geologic structure, a backroad of time and place and memory.

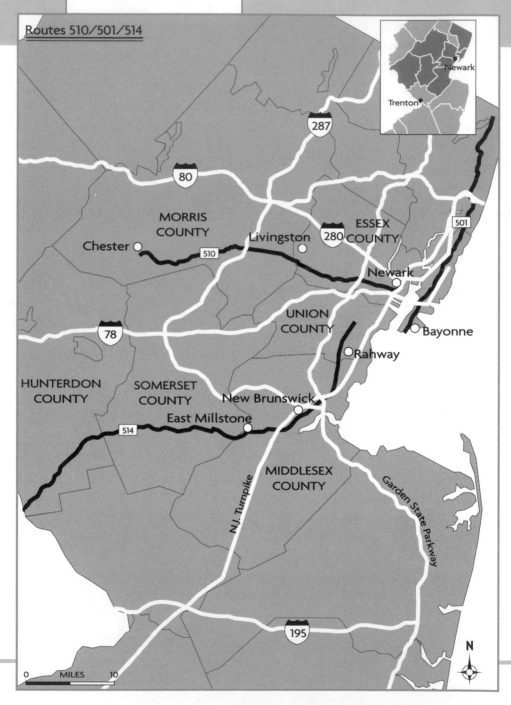

CHAPTER

TWO

Routes 510/501/514

Newark

Trenton

287

80

MORRIS
COUNTY

Chester

510

Livingston

280

ESSEX
COUNTY

501

Newark

78

UNION
COUNTY

Bayonne

Rahway

HUNTERDON
COUNTY

SOMERSET
COUNTY

New Brunswick

514

East Millstone

MIDDLESEX
COUNTY

N.J. Turnpike

Garden State Parkway

195

N

0   MILES   10

Routes 510, 501, and 514 have two things in common: they all begin in a congested urban-industrial center, go through miles of suburbs, and end in Small Town, New Jersey.

A drive along any of these roads is a timeline study of New Jersey's ongoing suburban expansion, or "sprawl" as it has become known in the last half of the twentieth century.

The word *sprawl* to many people is like the word *cancer*. Dreaded. Terminal. Without cure. But the truth is, not all growth is bad. Towns and lifestyles are changing, sure, but not always for the worse. Hospitals and schools get built. Utilities and services improve. Dying towns renew. And part of that renewal is traffic, noise, overcrowding, pollution, etc.

Sprawl is many things, good and bad.

But one thing sprawl is not is new.

These three roads show that the movement of bulk populations from city to country is no post–World War II phenomenon. Instead it begins with the railroads in the mid-1800s. It picks up speed with the opening of the Holland Tunnel (1927), the George Washington Bridge (1931), and the first tube of the Lincoln Tunnel (1937). Some of New Jersey's finest suburban towns and town sections—Essex Fells, Short Hills, Llewellyn Park, Upper Montclair, Morristown, Ridgewood, Summit, Westfield, Plainfield (in its day)—were built up in the middle to late 1800s—well before the automobile was a necessary household appliance. In the early part of the 1900s, these towns and others like them were expanded block by block, filled with sturdy, well-made, and architecturally tasteful homes on conforming lots, built for the middle class. (I remember two workers taking two days to knock down a wall for a kitchen expansion in my parents' c. 1920s Normandy Tudor in Summit. The walls were plaster over wire mesh over lathe over concrete.)

In the postwar years, more houses were punched out in Levittown fashion, with whole city sections of Cape Cods, ranches, and splits going up ricky-tick. Then came the housing stock boom in the 1970s and '80s to accommodate the baby-boom generation, who now had families of their own. The suburbs could no longer hold them, and with their sheer numbers and white-collar affluence, they created exurbia—turning formerly rural areas into high-end 'burbs of minimanses on three-acre lots.

No road in the state tells this complete story as 510 does.

There are two ways to look at 510, which begins in downtown Newark and ends thirty-one miles away in downtown Chester.

The most obvious way is to look at the beginning and end, and see the worlds-apart economic and social differences. Newark, beaten and blighted, staggering back from a half-century of decay. Chester, a thriving country village in the heart of one of the state's spreading wealth belts. Newark, black and Hispanic and poor. Chester, where being a minority means you only own one car. Using 510 as an asphalt spectrum, Newark and Chester couldn't be at more opposite ends.

But to see 510 as a story of two extremes is to miss all that lies in between.

Drive the whole road and see the ups and downs of downtown Newark, the ghosts of the Vailsburg section, the old English–style village of South Orange (part of the first wave of New Jersey suburban development), and the modern suburban sprawl of Livingston Township.

Drive the whole road and go through the old estate lands of Morris Township, now home to the well-manicured properties of corporate headquarters, through Morristown, with its colonial-age green and its lawyer-based economy, its historic side streets and classy restaurants, its citylike seediness germinating below the surface, and out to the decreasingly rural and increasingly exclusive Mendham and Chester.

Drive the whole road—and you visit many points along that line.

Like a series of museum dioramas, 510 showcases every archetype of urban, suburban, and exurban residential neighborhood and retail center of the last hundred years—some frozen in time by architecture, setting, or circumstance, others barely recognizable from a few short decades ago.

Route 510 is not simply the story of cities and suburbs. It's the story of how they evolve and change and sprawl, how neighborhoods change and how people shift, how centers of commerce and retail move. It is the story of urban, suburban, and rural renewal and decay, the endless cycle of property use and abuse.

Route 510 is not the story of distinct places and distinct points in time, nor is it the story of black and white. It is the story of how those places have changed—the shades of gray difficult to bring into focus without looking through the long lens of time.

Here's one example:

The old Bamberger's building on the corner of Market and Washington Streets in Newark was one of the busiest department stores in the world through the 1930s and 1940s. The block-long store sold everything—from ladies' fashions to hunting gear, including guns, for the outdoors enthusiasts. I remember shopping in "Bam's" with my family in the early sixties, and my mother using the store to get furniture re-upholstered into the next decade. Later it became Macy's, but by the 1980s, the granite titan with the decorative stone trim was closed. Its customer base had abandoned Newark for the suburbs, and Macy's itself joined the exodus, setting up anchor stores in the new indoor malls around the state—including Livingston Mall, also on 510. The world had changed around the store.

Then it changed again.

The Macy's building today is once again one of the busiest of its kind. This time the name brands aren't stamped on dresses and shoes and housewares, they're stamped on a billion dollars worth of telecommunications equipment. Macy's has become a major carrier hotel, its nine floors of retail space now rented out to telecom giants like IDT, Qwest, and MCI Worldcom. A carrier hotel is a place where companies such as these store their switching stations and computer servers—a warehouse for the worldwide phone network and the Internet. And while the new Macy's building doesn't attract legions of shoppers and the work force to serve them, it does bolster the city's growing reputation as a telecom center, a place with the infrastructure, fiber optics, and hard-wiring to lure new service businesses.

Downtown Newark may not be the bustling retail center it was in the 1930s and '40s, but it still brings in thousands of white-collar workers on two train lines and two interstates every day to jobs at places like Prudential, Horizon Blue Cross/Blue Shield, and Verizon (formerly New Jersey Bell), all Newark stalwarts. With big new employers like IDT and the credit company MBNA, the opening of the new Performing Arts Center, and the pending arena deal, life has been breathed back into a downtown left for dead after the riots in 1967 (see color plate 3).

4. Downtown Newark, March 2001.
Star-Ledger photo by Andrew Mills.

5. The Lincoln Memorial in front of the old Essex County Courthouse in downtown Newark.
Photo by Mark Di Ionno.

The road begins in one of the few unchanged parts of the city—the heavily Portuguese Ironbound, east of McCarter Highway.

First as Passaic Avenue, then as Raymond Boulevard, 510 forms the northern border of the Ironbound. The easternmost part of the road goes through a heavy industrial area and is clogged by tractor-trailers making their way to the New Jersey Turnpike and Routes 1 and 9. Going into the Ironbound, you see a northeastern cityscape from the early part of the twentieth century: well-maintained homes whose front-yard squares of grass display religious statues, bird baths, and planters, people on porch stoops or in lawn chairs on sidewalks on hot summer nights, mom-and-pop stores and restaurants—some now run by grandsons and grand-daughters—cars double-parked, children in fence-bound parks, the energy and controlled chaos of many people living cooperatively and safely in a small space.

The Ironbound today looks very much as Vailsburg must have looked in the mid-twentieth century. Here's a description from the *WPA Guide to 1930s New Jersey* (reprint; New Brunswick: Rutgers University Press, 1986): "In the northwestern part of the city are the Roseville and Vailsburg sections, which present old Newark with a suburban facing. Perhaps more than any other district, Roseville has a community sense, emphasized by homelike frame dwellings, strips of lawn and quiet streets. In Vailsburg . . . the prevalent housing unit is the two-family structure, set close to the curb and fronted with an iron rail."

Vailsburg, like many Newark neighborhoods on the west side of the downtown, has changed. The old synagogues have been converted into Baptist or nondenominational Christian churches, and some of the old Jewish cemeteries—one in the shadow of the shuttered Pabst beer plant—are overgrown and neglected, the descendants of the dead having moved on to places west on 510 like South Orange, Millburn, and Livingston. There are, in parts of Vailsburg, all the expected social ills of the city—drugs, derelicts, street crime, property neglect. But look closely and you can see some stubborn residuals of the old neighborhood—the stone-front houses that refuse to crumble, the tidy residential street here or there, children headed to school in their parochial school uniforms, the

6. A Jewish Cemetery in Vailsburg with the vacant Pabst Brewery in the background.
Photo by Mark Di Ionno.

raised-letter street signs that say "Historic Vailsburg." At Monticello and Longfellow Streets in Vailsburg are homes that look downright suburban, fitting in comfortably with the neighboring Colonials, Tudors, and Greek Revivals of South Orange.

There is another neighborhood on the west side of downtown that's changed, too.

Society Hill is a sprawling network of townhomes built on cul-de-sacs on both sides of 510 near the University of Medicine and Dentistry of New Jersey complex. This part of 510, called South Orange Avenue, was ground zero for the 1967 riots. For years afterward, much of the street remained shelled out, its blackened and vacant buildings and storefronts haunting reminders of the day the city went beyond the point of fore-seeable return.

Now there are neighborhoods. And the cul-de-sac—that much-hated builders' invention of the suburbs that proliferated in places like Florham Park twelve miles up 510—has found new respect in city plan-ning. At Society Hill, the cul-de-sac—blamed in the suburbs for every-thing from neighborhood alienation to the death of mass transit to the birth of strip malls—binds neighbors together in the city by helping

7. Society Hill, part of Newark's housing renewal.
Photo by Mark Di Ionno.

people look out for one another, cutting down on through (and transient) traffic, and giving kids a safe place to play.

If you consider Vailsburg a city-suburb hybrid, then South Orange is the first purely classic suburb west of Newark on 510.

South Orange, with its old Tudor mortar-and-beam city hall, brick-and-turreted firehouse, and slate-shingled train station, was built at a time when American architecture zeroed in on all things English. Like other towns in the cluster known as "Suburban Essex"—Montclair, Glen Ridge, Orange, East Orange, Maplewood, Millburn (Short Hills), Essex Fells, and Summit (even though it is in Union County)—the Village of South Orange is heavy on Victorian homes and Tudor public buildings, especially the schools. It is, simply, a beautiful town of beautiful homes, many of which are situated on the slopes of First Watchung Mountain.

Route 510 skirts part of Maplewood (South Orange's sister city) before cutting through the South Mountain Reservation in a twisty-turny road that engineers built as a tight two lanes each way but cut down to one in the last decade or so.

The reservation proves open space has been a Jersey issue for over a century. Back in 1895, Essex County bought nearly twenty-five hundred acres for parkland between the Watchung slopes and outside the rapidly growing 'burbs of the Oranges, Maplewood, and Millburn. It was a good thing. Back in 1895, the South Mountain and Eagle Rock Reservations were gateways to New Jersey's farm areas. Today they are islands of green in the spreading megalopolis.

Beyond the reservation, you see suburban development different from the cozy old towns to the east. You see sprawl circa the 1950s, 1960s, and 1970s. You see neighborhoods of cul-de-sacs with bigger houses and more land. You see shopping districts centralized not in downtowns but in clusters of strip malls and, of course, the Livingston Mall, one of the first enclosed shopping centers in the state. Where once there were isolated modest homes on the road, there is now a swirl of off-streets lined with ostentatious modern stone-faced homes. The McMansion developments of the rural counties have their roots here—when areas of Livingston and Short Hills used to be little more than farmland, and 510 a backroad connecting the Oranges with Morristown. In the vicinity of Livingston Mall on the Morris-Essex county border, 510 has exploded in the past fifteen years with a variety of corporate head-quarters, condo complexes, and large homes filling small lots in new res-idential neighborhoods.

That's not to say there is no natural beauty here.

From the top of Second Mountain, 510 begins a long descent into the flats between the Watchungs and the foothills of the Highlands. As with the views from 527 on this slope, this westward look is expansive—all sky, distant hills, and church steeples, with water towers and other land-mark buildings in between. When the clouds are feathery and scattered, or heavy and gathering—and especially at sunset—the sky here is open and glowing and a beautiful thing to behold.

In between this slope and the distant blue waves of hills are the wet-land remnants of Glacial Lake Passaic.

Glacial Lake Passaic—like Glacial Lake Hackensack, which we today call the Meadowlands—was formed by retreating mountains of ice that plugged the Passaic and Hackensack Rivers with rock debris, preventing them from draining eastward to the bays. The glaciers changed the course of the Passaic River. Instead of being able to flow through the rock-walled Hobart Gap (about two miles south of 510 between Short Hills and Summit), the Passaic cut through the lowlands west of the Sec-ond Watchung Mountain, heading up toward Little Falls and Paterson.

Glacial Lake Passaic was ten miles wide and thirty miles long, filling the valley between the Second Watchung and the Highlands to the west. The Great Swamp, about ten miles south of 510, was part of the geologic structure. Many of the areas closest to the Passaic River today are still prone to flooding; the wetlands you see from Routes 24, 80, and 280 in this vicinity—usually brimming in spring—are part of the swamps left by Glacial Lake Passaic.

The massive area today is a valuable watershed. In the immediate area of 510 are three large reservoirs built by the Commonwealth Water Company and a smaller body of water called Taylor Lake. The road crosses the fairly wide Canoe Brook, then the smaller Slough Brook, both tributaries of the Passaic River. The road also crosses the Passaic—which serves as the Morris-Essex county border—just west of the Livingston Mall. Past Florham Park, the road goes over another Passaic tributary called the Black Brook, and the wetlands surrounding are called Black Meadows.

When I was a college student—back before Route 24 was built through—I took 510 every day through Black Meadows at daybreak on my way to Rutgers in Newark. I remember how each morning the mist would cling to the swamp grass, tucked down between the low trees like a cottony quilt blanketing the landscape. The trees blocked the morning breeze, keeping the mist alive until the sun rose high enough to burn it off. Through this haze you could make out the shadows of deer, still as they grazed, or walking gingerly across the spongy ground. The road was straight and the tree line squat, so the sun had room to paint its muted colors on the morning sky—the nuances of orange, red and pink and blue, violet and gray that forecast the day. All this beauty and softness, I remember thinking, just four minutes from Morristown and thirty minutes from Newark. I think of this often when I tell my children, "Never let anyone tell you that you live in an ugly state." The landscape is naturally beautiful, and it changes rapidly enough to never be dull.

It was this natural beauty—and the availability of land and proximity to New York—that made the Morristown area a favored place of the privileged class for building estates from the 1880s to the 1910s. In 1900, one hundred millionaires were said to live within a mile radius of Morristown (see color plate 4).

Many lived on Madison Avenue (Route 124), which runs somewhat parallel with 510 as they angle toward Morristown. But there were a few on 510, most notably financier Otto Kahn, whose Cedar Crest estate on Columbia Road (now Columbia Turnpike, as 510 is known here) looked like a Miami South Beach resort complex. Kahn's estate is now the property of Allied Chemical, and only some stables converted into homes remain of the original buildings. Nearby, down what is now Park Avenue toward Madison, was the Florham, the estate of Hamilton Mckeon

Twombley and his wife, Florence (nee Vanderbilt), whose marriage combined two of America's richest families. The centerpiece of their estate was the hundred-ten-room mansion, which today is the administration building of Fairleigh Dickinson University. Some of the old Florham barns, converted into office space, can be seen along Park Avenue, and the FDU campus is filled with outbuildings, brick walls, entranceways, and stone decorations from the old estate.

In the vicinity of 510 (especially on Normandy Parkway and Normandy Heights Road), some of the old mansions still exist, most for corporate or institutional use. Whippany Farms, the estate of George Griswold Frelinghuysen, built in 1891, is now an arboretum and the headquarters of the Morris County Park Commission. The Peter Frelinghuysen mansion is now the Morris Museum. The mansion of Leland H. Ross, a Newark civil engineer, is now the main building at Bayley-Ellard, a Catholic high school. The mansion of banker William S. Thorne is now the Unitarian Church on Normandy Heights Road. Another on 510 is Acorn Hall, a Victorian Italianate mansion that is today the headquarters of the Morris County Historical Society (see color plate 5). Many others can be seen on Madison Avenue, converted into a variety of office condos or corporate headquarters.

The old wealth belt continues on the west side of Morristown, where 510 bends around the square and heads out of town as Washington Street and Mendham Road (also as Route 124 or old Route 24). There are two particularly notable old estates on this part of 510, going through an area known locally as Washington Valley. The former four-thousand-acre estate of banker Luther Kountze, with its stone centerpiece mansion known as Delbarton, is now a premier boys' Catholic prep school of the same name. Fosterfields, the Stick Style Victorian mansion built by the grandson of Paul Revere and once rented by nineteenth-century author Bret Harte, is now a working nineteenth-century farm run by the Morris County Parks.

Since this is a chapter about land use, I would be remiss not to mention the ongoing battle between environmentalists and the Benedictine monks who run Delbarton. The monks, saying they need to develop part of their land to ensure their future, plan to convert sixty acres into an assisted living facility. The property borders Jockey Hollow, part of the Morristown National Historic Park. The federal government once made a passing offer to buy the property, but the monks balked at the price. The line of critics teeing off on the monks for their "greed" is long: residents, environmentalists, the National Park Service. But in fairness to the monks, they *bought* the property in the 1920s, it was not gifted to them, and the fact that they have owned it all these years and kept it pristine is part of what has made this area so worth protecting.

Yes, this stretch of 510 is very pretty. The homes, when you can see them, are mostly picturesque, rambling colonial farmhouses, many with ponds on the property. The landscape is hilly, filled with open, sloping valleys that front distant mountain vistas.

I got to know this area intimately when I lived on Western Avenue in Morris Township, just a mile from the Morristown Green and three miles from the east entrance of Jockey Hollow.

In those days I spent a lot of time in Jockey Hollow and contiguous Lewis Morris Park, right off 510, running the trails, hiking with the kids, and in winter sleigh-riding or skating on the lake at Lewis Morris. As I write this, I realize I did none of it as much as I wanted, but I did enough to know the parks well. Jockey Hollow, especially, became and remains one of my favorite places in New Jersey. I wrote this about Jockey Hollow in December of 2000, as part of a *Star-Ledger* story on favorite winter places by a number of writers:

> In winter, the wind comes in volleys down the slopes of Jockey Hollow, creating whirlpools of dead leaves in the clefts of the hills.
>
> In the woods here are the echoes of history. In the shrill whistle of the wind, you can hear the fifes of the Continental Army infantry brigades as they drilled on the Grand Parade ground, which despite its grandiose name, is nothing more than a naked meadow. In the snap of the frozen branches on the wind-whipped trees, you can hear the crackling of the green wood in the hearth fires soldiers huddled around to keep warm. And when the wind's utterances deepen to an

icy growl, you can hear the groans of the men near starvation, dying of smallpox and exposure.

"Dead Carcasses in and about Camp are to be buried by fatigue parties from the Brigade near which they lay," Washington wrote on Feb. 20, 1780, in his general orders.

Jockey Hollow in winter is a cold place with a history of misery. The hardships endured there in the brutal winter of 1779–80 are legendary. Many of the soldiers wrapped rags around their feet for shoes. . . .

. . . In the hills of Jockey Hollow, you can see how the soldiers lived. Small, dirt-floored, wooden huts slept eight. The rough-hewn planks may slow the wind, but the cold penetrates and is everywhere. You think of the history, and the misery, and shiver.

I also came to know Fosterfields on 510 during this time of my life, not as a place of recreation, but of work—well, sort of.

I was part of the college-kid gang that worked for the Morris County parks in summer, and I was assigned to Fosterfields. This was county work, where the common greeting among us in our forest green tee shirts was "Working hard or hardly working?"

It was usually the latter. We spent eight hours a day, from 8 a.m. to 4 p.m., cutting grass, clearing brush, and otherwise manicuring Fosterfields and the parts of Patriot's Path nearby.

In those days, the late 1970s, Fosterfields was only partially open for business. The interpretive center was up and running, but the mansion was closed and many of the fields still needed to be cleared. We spent many days hacking and sawing, and throwing wood into the industrial chipper, an angry machine that would suck branches through and reduce them to wood chips. You could feel the power of the chipper, especially when a branch got entangled in your shirtsleeve and the teeth of the chipper tugged at your arm. (So you know, I am typing this with two hands and ten fingers.) We also spent many days riding lawn tractors or pushing mowers, sometimes going over and over grass already cut to make ourselves look busy.

One day we finished cutting at 3:30. The other college kid and I started having a catch. A parks commissioner came by and saw us and complained to our supervisor, a county lifer, who was in the shed making some cages for his backyard, where he kept a small collection of birds and rodents.

"Next time, look busy," he said.

A few days later, we again finished early and we shut the machines down.

"Start 'em up and keep moving," he said.

The other college kid, the other full-time lifer on our crew, and I walked in circles around the interpretive center for the next half-hour. At 4 p.m., the supervisor came out and gave us the signal—a finger across the throat—to shut down. The other college kid and I shut off our engines. The lifer was in front of us still pushing, but his machine was quiet. He never turned his back on.

"Why waste the gas?" he explained. "If somebody came by, they would never know it wasn't on. Three lawn mowers going sound the same as two going, right?"

Another day we spent from eight till ten in the morning watching the flight of crows, trying to figure out where their nest was. The supervisor wanted a crow for his backyard bird menagerie, and the best way to get one was to steal a baby from its nest.

"They're sneaky bastards," the supervisor said of the adult crows as we sat in the county pickup truck, watching them perch, then fly around, over and over in a variety of trees. "They go from tree to tree to tree. They never go back to their nests right away because they're scavengers and raid other birds' nests. They know the other birds will attack their nests to get even."

After two hours of watching crows, the supervisor said. "That's it. That tall evergreen in there. That's where the nest is."

He started the pickup, drove fifty feet, looked at his watch and said, "Whaddaya know? Break time already," and shut the truck back off.

We had a break, then spent the rest of the morning planning a strategy and gathering tools for the assault on the nest. In the afternoon, the

8. Downtown Chester on an early spring day.
Star-Ledger photo by George Baumann.

supervisor, properly belted and spiked, went up the tree to cut down the branch that held the nest.

"If anybody comes by, tell 'em we're trimming broken branches," he said.

"But there's no broken branches," I said.

"Not yet," he said.

By the end of the afternoon, he had his baby crow.

This stretch of 510 is the gateway to the Mendhams and Chesters, formally rural in many areas and now increasingly exclusive. The road here winds through mixed areas of old estates and luxury home developments of different vintages. Downtown Mendham dates back architecturally to the colonial period, with the in-town homes all converted to things like real-estate, architecture, and law offices.

Outside Mendham, the road dips and bends and rises, continuing to take you past some of the most desirable real estate in New Jersey. This is exurbia—affluence with a rural flavor—big homes on big land that costs big money, the American Dream at its big-screen best. This is not cookie-cutter, cul-de-sac suburban sprawl. This is five- or ten-acre zoning sprawl. Sprawl that brings fewer houses and fewer people, but sprawl just the same. And the Land Rover wealth of these new residents is trimming the rough edges from our rural areas.

Case in point:

For years, there was flea market at Chester—the old-fashioned kind with rows of vendors selling antiques, handmade crafts, an assortment of junk and seconds, mass-produced crafts that were supposed to look handmade, and things that fell off the truck or through the cracks at the warehouse. It was dusty and hot, and filled with operators looking to separate the fat ladies in stretch pants from their money.

This sense of entrepreneurial anarchy, fused with the growing wealth of the area, began to transform downtown Chester into a collection of crafts and antique stores—not aimed at fat ladies in stretch pants but at slim ladies (with fat wallets) in weekend Ralph Lauren jeans. Downtown Chester (510) was suddenly one four-block stretch of country boutiques, drawing the gentry and gentry wannabes from all over. Downtown Chester was no longer agri-authentic—the hardware, grain, and general stores now sold decorations, not necessities—it was something else, an upscale facsimile of what it once had been.

Now the flea market and country boutique crowds converged. Weekend traffic became unbearable. Something had to go.

Guess which?

The flea market is now in Dover.

Think of it. . . .

Upscale Chester today is perhaps as alien to the old-time rural folk there as present-day downscale Newark is to people who remember when it buzzed with "Bam's" and Hahnes and the other stores along Broad and Market.

Things change. Something gets lost, something gets left behind. That is the story of 510—that, and everything in between.

Like 510, Route 501 starts in an urban area and travels through city and suburb, but the change is not as gradual, and the road does not go through such a varied economic, geographic, and historic landscape. Route 501 is John F. Kennedy Boulevard from Bayonne, where it starts, through Jersey City, Union City, and the waterfront Hudson County towns, before hooking up through Palisades Park and Englewood as Grand Avenue. North of Englewood, it becomes an old Bergen County main line, linking the old suburbs of Cresskill, Demarest, Closter, and Rockleigh as it runs parallel to the Palisades before exiting into New York's Rockland County. This road is certainly worth the ride—and a study in the state's changing demographics.

Like 510, 501 has places frozen in time. Bayonne, still blue-collar, still white in the European immigrant way, is a tight-knit community of mom-and-pop stores and ethnic enclaves. On the north end of the highway, the old Bergen suburbs remain what they were. They are increasingly affluent, yes, but they still have enough townies to make them places many generations have called home. These are all New Jersey small towns, as comfortable and familiar—and maybe as boring—to those who have grown up there as the villages and hamlets of the rural counties south and west.

In between lies the melting pot. Jersey City, settled in the 1600s by Dutch traders, has been transformed many times over in industry and ethnicity. In Union City, where ethnic tensions were once between old, industrial-based whites and Hispanics, tensions are now between Hispanics and Asians. The Hispanics now recite an all-too-familiar American refrain: they feel like foreigners in their own neighborhoods, as the influx of Asian peoples and Asian-owned businesses creates a whirl of languages and customs they don't understand. Up the line, in Palisades Park, Koreans have led a triple-digit percentage rise in the number of Asians between the 1990 and 2000 censuses, as Cubans and Hispanics did in Union City and North Bergen a generation ago. This is the recurring story of urban New Jersey, repopulated every generation by a new ethnic group looking to make a better life and move on up the road.

————

Route 514, too, is worth the ride—if only for the incongruity of its industrial beginning and rural end.

For the record, 514 was not included as a separate segment of this book simply because it is a confusing case of missing signs on the eastern end. It is congested through Linden, where it is Elizabeth Avenue, then tough to follow. It is East Grand Avenue for a block in Rahway, then Rahway Avenue into Woodbridge. After a few frustrating twists through Woodbridge Center, it continues as Woodbridge Avenue through Fords, Edison, and Highland Park. It merges briefly with Route 27, then gets lost again in the maze of downtown New Brunswick. It becomes Hamilton Avenue and stays that way through New Brunswick and the grim Somerset section of Franklin Township. The road's transformation into a suburban-country road is somewhat abrupt—you are surrounded by parks, golf courses, and historic homes as the road becomes Amwell Road. This area is growing, and the infrastructure is being laid down to accommodate the population increase. The road is freshly widened, with new curbing and big, two-lane intersections with stoplights. On each side of 514, ground is being broken for housing developments.

The road goes into the East Millstone section of Franklin Township, a worse-for-wear historic district that seems more distant from mainstream New Jersey than it really is—it is less than ten miles from downtown New Brunswick. This pocket of the old town spans the old Delaware and Raritan Canal and the Millstone River. The Franklin Inn, a former stage stop where British General Cornwallis stayed during the Revolution, is now a bookstore run by the non-profit Meadows Foundation, a Somerset County historical group.

This New Jersey backroad countryside doesn't last long. Through Hillsborough, 514 looks like a line of demarcation for suburban sprawl.

Case in point: across 514 from Yablonski's Stock Farm and the brown-and-white cows huddled near the barns, is a regional office for

9. Yablonski's Stock Farm on 514.
Photo by Mark Di Ionno.

RCN Cable TV company with a giant antenna towering over the road. Beyond the junction of 514 and Route 206, you get the feeling the Hillsborough town leaders have never rejected a blueprint. There are two brand-new shopping centers surrounded by a dense cluster of attached-housing units. Down the road, single-family houses take over, with mid-scale developments springing up out of farmland (see color plate 6). In some cases, the old barns and silos are still on the property, silent witnesses to the ringing of hammers echoing through the valley and the wood frames being raised on cinder foundations with assembly-line rhythm. For miles of 514 through Hillsborough, the pattern continues. Farmland turns into homes, homes into neighborhoods. Not better or worse, just different. One lifestyle goes, another comes in. For the children in these new neighborhoods this land, too, will always be home, just as it has been for the generations of farm children before them. Does growing up in a subdivision make childhood memories any less precious?

In a village like East Millstone or Neshanic or Ringoes, both down the road on 514, things and faces stay the same because there is no land to build on in the village proper, and these are rural hometowns people don't want to leave. But out in the rolling countryside, there is room to grow, room for new people to come in and build up a new suburban hometown of their own, room for family memories and experiences, room for neighborhoods to form, room for people to live out their American dream.

CHAPTER
THREE

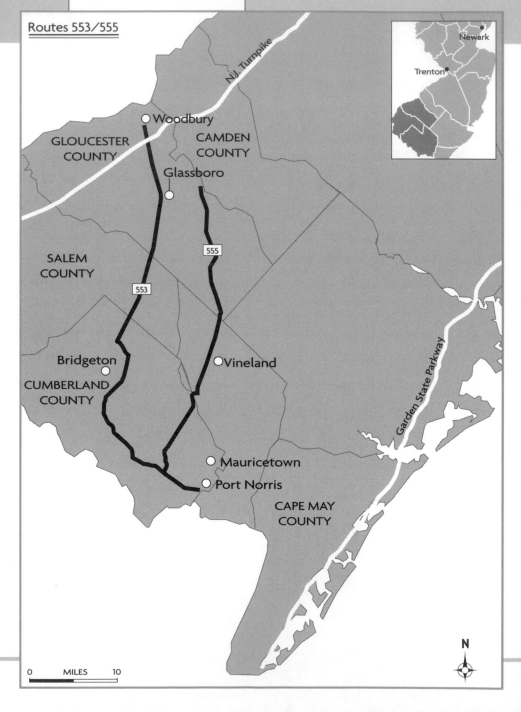

Routes 553/555

Woodbury
GLOUCESTER COUNTY
CAMDEN COUNTY
Glassboro
N.J. Turnpike
SALEM COUNTY
555
553
Bridgeton
CUMBERLAND COUNTY
Vineland
Garden State Parkway
Mauricetown
Port Norris
CAPE MAY COUNTY

Newark
Trenton

0   MILES   10

N

What constitutes South Jersey?

It is a question demographers and social scientists have kicked around since the East and West Jerseys of colonial times were unified into modern-day New Jersey. And the answer proves to be as elusive and illogical as understanding why someone who calls Jersey home roots for the Phillies instead of the Yanks.

The definitions of South Jersey depend on who you talk to, and where they are from. For people in Newark, Trenton is South Jersey. For people in Trenton, Salem is South Jersey. For people in Salem, Trenton is North Jersey. People in Trenton say they're from Central Jersey, which few people from North and South Jersey recognize as a real place.

People in Phillipsburg say they're from West Jersey. People in Pennsville, who are farther west than Phillipsburg by twenty miles, say they're from South Jersey. To people in Pennsville, there is no such place as West Jersey. It's all North Jersey, unless it's South Jersey, or the Shore.

The Shore makes South Jersey's eastern border just as nebulous as its northern border. The Shore starts in midstate, on the Raritan Bay. People in Atlantic Highlands, ten miles down the bay, say they're from the Shore, as does everyone else on the coast from there all the way down to Cape May. People in Cape May don't say they're from South Jersey. They say they're from the Shore. So do people on Long Beach Island, in Toms River, on Point Pleasant, in Belmar, and all the way up to the Shore town of Highlands.

So what is South Jersey?

Some say it's New Jersey's bottom eight counties—Atlantic, Burlington, Camden, Cape May, Cumberland, Gloucester, Ocean, and Salem—but there are some flaws to that thinking. Much of Ocean, because of population migration, leans toward New York. Northern Burlington is in the Trenton metro area, thus being neither North nor South. And the Shore, as stated, is simply the Shore.

Whatever South Jersey is, there is no dispute that Routes 553 and 555 run through the heart of it. Beginning in the Philly suburb of Woodbury, 553 heads due south, connecting the metro area with the Pitman-Glassboro region, and goes from there into the farmlands of Pittsgrove and the Deerfields, skirting Bridgeton, crossing the Cohansey at Fairton, then following the coast of Delaware Bay to Port Norris and the Maurice River.

Route 555 intersects with 553 at Dividing Creek and heads north through the Bear Swamp East Natural Area and the Millville Wildlife Management Area. The road runs alongside the scenic Maurice River, a thick meandering artery surrounded by swaying, golden grass, into Millville and Vineland, cutting through the most productive twenty miles of farm soil in the state.

Routes 553 and 555 form an eighty-five mile loop through Gloucester, Salem, and Cumberland counties, which, by any definition, is all South Jersey. And it is these roads that finally make clear what South Jersey is. They show you, north to south, the four distinct aspects of South Jersey: the burgeoning suburban growth south of Philadelphia at Woodbury, Woodbury Heights, and Wenonah; the rich and expansive agricultural belt with its weathered centers like Pitman and Vineland; the sagging industrial centers of Bridgeton and Millville; and the hunting and fishing paradise and maritime traditions of the bay side.

In this South Jersey, you will find:

— The nineteenth-century ship captains' community in Mauricetown.

— Greenwich, the most undisturbed and unknown colonial village in New Jersey, site of the Greenwich Tea Party, the first overtly anti-British act in the colony.

— Endless fields of green, leafy plants around Vineland, where farming is an industrial-sized business that runs the local economy, watered by monstrous irrigation machines that look like something out of *War of the Worlds*.

—— The vacant factories and the glorious old houses crumbling under the weight of Bridgeton's gloomy poverty. Bridgeton, with twenty-two hundred standing homes built in the colonial, Federalist, and Victorian eras, has the largest historic district in New Jersey—bigger than Cape May, much bigger than Princeton. What it does not have is the elegant panache of those places. Instead it is more like a Plainfield: an architectural and historic gem flawed by certain cruelties of the times—crime, drugs, and poverty. Bridgeton's turnaround in many neighborhoods is more complete than Plainfield's, and many of its people are optimistic about restoring it to its rightful place among New Jersey's most historic towns.

—— Thundergut Pond, one of the nearly one hundred Wildlife Management Areas in the bay area.

—— The loneliness of Finn's Point National Cemetery, the final mass resting place for some twenty-five hundred Confederate soldiers who died at Fort Delaware, the Andersonville of the North.

—— The eeriness of the Hancock House, scene of a Revolutionary War massacre. The brick house stands today, but efforts to open it as a museum have sputtered for decades, as if the dead want to be left alone.

—— Muskrat dinners—featuring real muskrats—used as fund-raisers for volunteer fire departments and ambulance corps throughout Salem and Cumberland counties (see color plate 7).

—— Miles and miles of empty road cutting through the farm fields, with their straight and endless rows of growing produce, their warehouse-sized storage bins and industrial-strength silos and fertilizer containers, and their shacklike dormitories for migrant workers. Miles and miles of empty road cutting through the scrub forests and grassy marshlands of the bay area, dead-ending at deserted beaches or the desolate swamps of the many wildlife preserves. Miles and miles of empty road connecting little out-of-the-way towns—centuries-old houses (some sagging, some restored), general stores, volunteer fire departments, and downtown steepled churches—places that haven't changed with the times

10. Fort Mott
State Park in
Salem County.
Star-Ledger photo
by Patti Sapone.

and don't want to. Villages where people turn to eyeball a strange car, but aren't unfriendly. Villages glad to be discovered, happy to share their history.

As I write this, I can't wait to go back.

I discovered South Jersey in two stages.

The first stage was in the mid-1970s, when I got stationed at the U.S. Navy Medical Center in South Philadelphia.

This seemed like a bad joke. During Hospital Corps School in Great Lakes, Illinois, we had to put in four choices for permanent duty. My first

Plate 1. The Ukrainian Orthodox Church.
Photo by Mark Di Ionno.

Plate 2. The Faith Bible Church on 527 in South Jersey.
Photo by Mark Di Ionno.

Plate 3. The old
Paramount Theater
in Newark.
Photo by Mark Di Ionno.

Plate 4. The George Washington
statue across from the
Ford Mansion in Morristown.
Star-Ledger photo
by Robert Sciarrino.

Plate 5. Acorn Hall in Morristown.
Photo by Mark Di Ionno.

Plate 6. The changing Somerset County countryside on 514.
Photo by Mark Di Ionno.

Plate 7. Frying muskrat at the Salem Rotary Club.
Star-Ledger photo by Matt Rainey.

Plate 8. Birds take flight over Fortescue.
Star-Ledger photo by Andrew Mills.

Plate 9. The dam at Union Lake in Millville.
Star-Ledger photo by Andrew Mills.

Plate 10. The Pine Barrens.
Photo by Mark Di Ionno.

Plate 11. A Pine Barrens forest fire.
Star-Ledger photo by Andrew Mills.

Plate 12. Harvesting cranberries.
Star-Ledger photo by Richard Raska.

Plate 13. A look at the canal on 533, south of Princeton.
Photo by Mark Di Ionno.

Plate 14. Apple Rose Farm on 537.
Photo by Mark Di Ionno.

Plate 15. Hessian soldiers fire away at the annual Battle of Monmouth reenactment.
Star-Ledger photo by Noah Addis.

Plate 16. Fall on Route 511 in Boonton Township.
Photo by Mark Di Ionno.

Plate 17. The Taylortown Reservoir on Route 511.
Photo by Mark Di Ionno.

Plate 18. A nursery in Middle Valley on Route 513.
Photo by Mark Di Ionno.

Plate 19. The bridge over the South Branch at Califon.
Photo by Mark Di Ionno.

Plate 20. A farm on the way to Pottersville.
Photo by Mark Di Ionno.

Plate 21. Mount Tammany.
Photo by Mark Di Ionno.

Plate 22. Old railroad tunnel on 519 in Warren County.
Photo by Mark Di Ionno.

Plate 23. Fred Space
with the late Goliath.
Star-Ledger photo by
Dorab Khandalavala.

Plate 24. The Lots of Time
Shop on 519 in Rosemont.
Photo by Mark Di Ionno.

Plate 25. The High Point Monument.
Star-Ledger photo by Robert Sciarrino.

choice was the North Atlantic, because I hoped to see Scotland, Ireland, Britain, and Scandinavia. My second choice was the Mediterranean, where I could put ashore in southern Europe, North Africa, and the Middle East. My third choice was Camp Lejeune. If I wasn't going to be a world traveler, then I could be a combat medic assigned to the Marines. My fourth choice was Philadelphia. I figured that would never happen.

It happened. In those days, the navy ad campaign was "Join the navy and see the world." And here I was, shipping off to a base just over the Walt Whitman Bridge from South Jersey.

For part of my four-year hitch, I lived off base in South Jersey, in a rooming house in Woodbury and then in an apartment in West Deptford, because the rents were cheaper than in Philadelphia. And because it was easier to keep a car.

Woodbury reminded me of a Midwest county seat. A little busy, a little rundown; a town with two distinct populations, the local banker-and-lawyer set, and the people, mostly rural types, who lived there to be near the social services. It struck me as backward and much less sophisticated than the New York area.

After spending my first year living on base, I had seen what I wanted of Philadelphia. In South Jersey, I had the freedom on nights and weekends to leave the city and the navy behind. My travels took me generally in three directions—out along Route 42 and the Atlantic City Expressway toward the Shore, or down Route 295 to areas along the Delaware River, or straight out 553 to Glassboro, where I had a friend at the college.

These were fairly uneventful explorations. Drive out, find a bar or a place to eat, drive back. But in discovering this part of New Jersey—be it in the shadows of the oil refineries along the river, or along the straight state highways lined with squat motels and strip malls, or in the old sleepy towns with block after block of simple frame houses—I realized I was a stranger in my home state. Almost everyone I met had no idea where I was from. North Jersey was as foreign to them as South Jersey was to me.

I was struck by three major differences between us (north) and them (south).

First, there were very few towns that looked like the part of New Jersey I had grown up in. Moorestown and Haddonfield had that finer-suburb polish, but almost everywhere else was more congested and rough around the edges.

Second, it didn't take as long to get into the hinterlands. In North Jersey, you could go through town after town of varying suburban cast, but it took a long time to get to the middle of nowhere. There were very few places within an hour of New York that counted as rural. In South Jersey, in those days, the Philly metro area was much smaller. Within fifteen minutes of the Walt Whitman Bridge, you could be in the country. This has changed in the last twenty years, certainly, and South Jersey is sprawling east and south of Philadelphia. But the metro region is still significantly smaller than New York's. For instance: Thirty miles dead east of the Walt Whitman Bridge are the sticks of Burlington County, the western edge of the Pine Barrens. Thirty miles dead west of the Lincoln Tunnel to Manhattan is the rather cosmopolitan suburb of Morristown.

Third, there were no mountains. South Jersey was basically flat—an inner coastal plain of fertile soil and sedimentary rock. There was nothing like the weathered granite hills of the Kittatinnys or the jagged traprock outcrops of the Watchungs. From the top of the Walt Whitman Bridge heading into South Jersey, sky met flat land—flat enough for you to see a storm roll in, flat enough to see a lightning strike a county away, flat enough to see a great expanse of sky—as flat as some northern plains state.

I admit all this was a paltry bit of knowledge. It was during my second stage of South Jersey wanderings, more than fifteen years later, that I began to appreciate the cultural differences, and how rich South Jersey is in folklore and craft, how much it resembles the Delmarva peninsula in mindset and even language. I found this by exploring the depths of the South, driving into places like Port Norris and Mauricetown and Greenwich, for a series of articles for the *Star-Ledger*, and later my first book, *New Jersey's Coastal Heritage*.

For one series in the paper, I explained exactly how far south South Jersey is:

If you stand on the bay side of Cape May County and look west from the shores of Town Bank, Fishing Creek, or Miami Beach, you are just a shade north of Covington, Kentucky.

Go a few miles up the coast to Reeds Beach and you are latitudinally even with Winchester, Virginia. Head up into Port Norris, and you are still south of Wheeling, West Virginia. Even Glassboro—fifty-five miles north of Port Norris on 553—would have been south of the Mason-Dixon line had it extended into New Jersey.

A segment of that series discussed the agriculture of South Jersey, which is in evidence for much of Route 553:

Farming is still big business in Cumberland and Salem. There aren't many mom-and-pop roadside stands; instead there are giant warehouses and industrial grain silos, dormitories for farm workers and miles of fertile fields filled with monster farm tractors and irrigation sprinklers.

Not surprisingly, the area spawned three food-related innovations that changed the way the world eats.

In 1858, Vineland's John Mason, a tinsmith, patented the Mason jar and produced it with the help of one of South Jersey's multitude of glass manufacturers, Samuel Crowley. Mason's screw-on lid created a vacuum in the jar, giving cooked or pickled foods a seemingly infinite shelf-life in the days before refrigeration.

As Mason's invention was becoming a standard item in kitchens everywhere, a Methodist minister in Vineland set out to tackle another problem. In 1869, the Rev. A. K. Street, who had strong reservations about serving an alcoholic beverage to Communion participants in his church, asked Dr. Thomas B. Welch, a Vineland dentist and grape-growing hobbyist, to find a grape-based substitute for wine. When other Methodist ministers found out about the grape juice sans alcohol, they asked Welch to supply them, too. Welch gave up his practice, bought two power presses and began to supply the church community. Welch next developed a way to bottle the juice to keep it fresh for long-distance shipping to churches beyond South

11. A diked riverfront farm in Cumberland County.
Star-Ledger photo by Andrew Mills.

Jersey. In 1896, Welch and his son, Charles, began a national advertising campaign to take Welch's Grape Juice from the sacristy to the kitchen tables of America. The campaign worked and the Welches moved the company from Vineland to New York State, where its product line expanded into the jellies and the other grape-based goods it continues to make today.

At about the same time, Arthur Seabrook was building his fifty-seven-acre farm, which sold produce locally, into a large growing concern that sent fresh fruits and vegetables to markets in New York, Baltimore, and Philadelphia. His son, Charles, took over management of the farm in 1912, and ten years later, it was a three-thousand-acre operation with a cannery and a cold storage plant. A few years later, Seabrook helped Clarence Birdseye refine the process for quick-freezing vegetables, and the world of frozen foods was opened up to consumers. Although the original company was sold (and the new owners left the frozen vegetable business), a new Seabrook Brothers and Sons, Incorporated, processes 65 million pounds of frozen vegetables a year for Birdseye and other private labels.

This capacity for growing brought trouble during the American Revolution.

Not too far from Seabrook's on 553 is the Centerton Inn (established in 1706), the oldest continuously operating inn in the state, and the second oldest in America. The inn was once a British customs office, and legend has it that here Gen. Anthony Wayne planned the foraging raids on South Jersey farms to feed the American army at Valley Forge during the winter of 1777–78. The British mistakenly thought the farmers were cooperating with Wayne, and sent down a raiding party of their own. On March 18, a battle at Quinton's Bridge (five miles east of Salem on what today is Route 49) resulted in about forty American casualties. Three days later, British forces stormed the home of Loyalist William Hancock and bayoneted twenty more militiamen, who had taken the house and were sleeping there. The brick house, with a zigzag pattern and Hancock's initials laid in near the roofline, is a state historic site, but keeps irregular hours. Mostly, visitors are greeted with a "closed until further notice" sign.

My travels through South Jersey for the *Star-Ledger* made me realize that I couldn't write a true book about the New Jersey Shore without including the Delaware Bay. From the tip of Cape May to the Salem-Gloucester border, the bay and river account for nearly one hundred miles of coast, only about thirty less than the Atlantic Coast from Sandy Hook to Cape May. This expanse of land could not be ignored—the maritime culture was as strong along the bay as on the ocean, and much of it still exists, hanging with the same briny stubbornness in the face of changing economies and depleted fisheries. The bay side has everything the ocean side has: lighthouses and boatyards, the lure and lore of ship life. Bayside history, in fact, is better preserved, because the recreational use of the bay is somewhat limited to fishing and hunting. The bay, with few sandy beaches, has not been overrun by motels, amusement parks, and summer cottages. Traffic on the bayside is usually a pickup truck carrying two unshaven buddies, dragging a boat—and easily passed on the straight, flat, and empty roads of the bay area.

Route 553 turns just north of Fortescue Island, the sportfishing capital of the Delaware Bay (see color plate 8). In the 1920s, it was called the Croaker Capital of the East Coast, and it attracted hordes of fishing enthusiasts from Philadelphia and South Jersey. In the 1980s, it was known as the Weakfish Capital of the World. Fortescue—which can be wholly seen from the one sand-and-stone road that loops through it—has seven marinas that dock everything from rented rowboats to fifty-five-foot party boats that hold fifty anglers. The largest marina is Higbee's, and the proprietor has a name right out of old salt central casting—Bunky Higbee.

"Around 1980 the weakfish hit their peak," Bunky told me a few years ago. "Guys were going out and coming home with two or three coolers full. . . . You couldn't get a parking space in town if you got here late. The boats were almost always full."

In the 1920s, the croakers were so plentiful that Fortescue had ten small hotels, which stayed booked all summer. That was the heyday, and while business is still good, it could be better.

"Almost everyone opens the first week of May and closes after Columbus Day weekend," Bunky said. "We don't close because there's no fish, we close because there's no people. There's plenty of fishing, but television's got everybody convinced summer ends on Labor Day" (see color plate 9).

Just east of Fortescue at the end of 553 is Port Norris, once known as the Oyster Capital of the World (the bay folks are not given to understatement).

The oyster beds of the Delaware Bay were once so full that there were twenty-nine processing plants and shipping companies in the Port Norris area. Now there is one. Fifty years ago, there were five hundred oyster boats working in the area. Now, only a few old-timers hold on. Those old-timers remember the hundred-car freight trains that headed north with the daily oyster harvest. Now the only whistle you hear is the wind through the marsh grass.

It all changed in 1957, when a disease known as MSX wiped out the oyster beds. The Port Norris oyster industry went from a $6-million-a-year business (in 1950s dollars) that employed forty-five hundred people and shaped the cultural landscape, to the ghost of trade and lifestyle, a memory kept by one company and a few family-run boats.

Other factors conspired to keep the industry down—pollution, recurring oyster diseases, and government warnings that oyster consumption could cause illness—and some of the oyster gatherers became crabbers instead.

The wharf area is also home to the Rutgers Oyster Research Lab, the *A. J. Meerwald*, a restored full sail schooner, and the Delaware Bay Schooner Center. The *Meerwald* plied the bay in the early part of the twentieth century, then was left to rot in the Maurice River. In 1988, Meghan Wren, then twenty-three and a veteran of boatyard work in Greenwich and Dorchester, began a campaign to save the vessel and started the Delaware Bay Schooner Project. An army of volunteers, including professional shipwrights, helped restore the ship over the next few years at a cost close to $750,000. The *Meerwald* now does educational and environmental sails on the bay, and is a frequent billowing participant in Tall Ship parades around the East Coast.

The center museum looks like an old mariner's attic, filled with oil-paintings of schooners, the antique tools of sailmaker Ed Cobb, the workbench of oyster basketmaker Noah Newcomb, and thousands of pictures of the old industry.

Upriver from Port Norris and not far from 553 is Mauricetown, which was home to eighty-nine sea captains between 1846 and 1915, the boom years of the shipping industry on the Maurice River. The yards built oyster boats, coastal schooners, and barge-type boats to carry the cordwood and cedar logs that were harvested in the area. The captains piloted up and down the Atlantic, from Newfoundland to South America. At the Mauricetown Episcopal Church on Noble Street, a stained-glass

12. Hull launch of the *A. J. Meerwald* on September 12, 1995.
Photo by George Schupp.

window installed in 1921 memorializes the twenty-two Mauricetown captains lost at sea.

There is a museum quality to Mauricetown, although the history is living, not glass-encased. The captains' houses at Mauricetown remain as private homes; the river remains full of boats of varying sizes. Like Greenwich in Salem County, Mauricetown is an authentic South Jersey town preserved not for posterity or prosperity but because the people who live there like it that way.

The culture and pace of Greenwich, Mauricetown, and many other small towns deep in South Jersey on Routes 553 and 555 is something gone from the New York and Philadelphia metro regions of the state. The comfort factor keeps people there, attached to a place they have known as home for generations.

13. Captain's house in Mauricetown.
Photo by Mark Di Ionno.

Perhaps this is why the Down Jersey Folklife Center at Wheaton Village exhibits not only the old-time crafts but the South Jersey people who raised those crafts to an art form. People like octogenarian Tom Brown of Millville, the last of the fur trappers; Barbara Fiedler of Pleasantville, who makes coiled pine needle baskets; the late Alexander Gustavis of Vineland, South Jersey's best-known basketmaker; the late Noah Newcomb of Dividing Creek, an oyster-basket-making legend; the noted boat builder John Dubois, an oyster boat captain and shipyard owner who has a museum filled with his stuff and named after him in Greenwich; Charlie Hankins of Lavalette, who made the Sea Bright skiff, a fishing/lifeguard boat designed to pound through surf.

"This center is about people, not products," director Jack Shortlidge told me a few years back. "These crafts, their work, goes to the very essence of who they are."

And where they live.

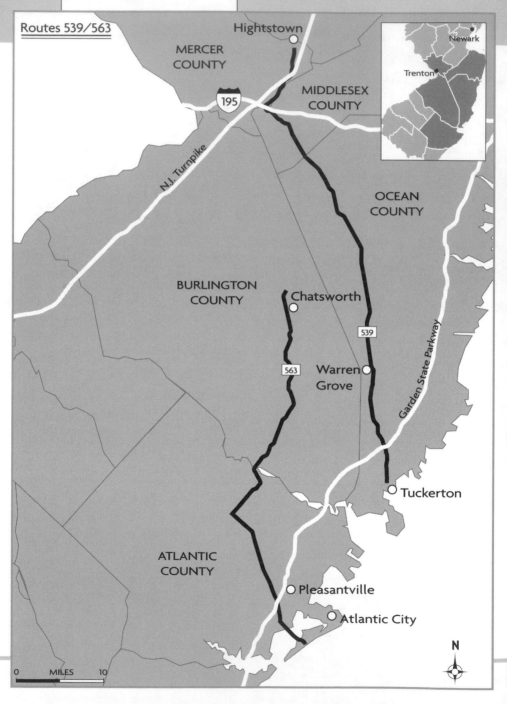

Routes 539/563

Hightstown

MERCER COUNTY

MIDDLESEX COUNTY

195

N.J. Turnpike

OCEAN COUNTY

BURLINGTON COUNTY

Chatsworth

539

563

Warren Grove

Garden State Parkway

Tuckerton

ATLANTIC COUNTY

Pleasantville

Atlantic City

Newark

Trenton

0   MILES   10

N

Together, Routes 539 and 563 add up to one hundred and five miles of flat road through the Pine Barrens, cranberry bogs, and salt-water marshes of the Jersey Shore. For miles and miles and miles on both roads, the only sign of civilization is the pavement itself and the occasional car coming in the opposite direction.

Welcome to New Jersey, the natural state. The New Jersey of pitch pines and white cedar, of stubby oaks and laurels (see color plate 10). Of forest critters like the southern flying squirrel, the southern bog lemming, the long-tailed weasel, and the gray fox. Of dozens of varieties of reptiles and amphibians, from the six-foot black rat snake to the two-inch four-toed salamander. Of more than one hundred species of birds and waterfowl, from the mighty bald eagle to the tiny redbreasted nuthatch.

In geologic terms this is the outer coastal plain: a spongy mish-mosh of consolidated sand, gravel, and other sedimentary materials deposited by the ocean and rivers or washed off the harder-surfaced areas to the north over the ages.

The two roads run through the heart of the forest-fire capital of the East Coast. The soil is so porous that water drains through the forest floor litter of leaves and pine needles, making them bone-dry kindling for the kind of fires that rack up destruction in square miles, rather than acres. Each year, fires of substantial anger churn through the Pine Barrens, leaving charcoaled trees and parched earth behind. It is a function of nature as much as humanity—a seasonal cleaning of the understory that makes the botanical survivors stronger (see color plate 11).

The porous soil makes the region one of the most valuable aquifers in the world—a seventeen-trillion-gallon underground lake of a thousand square miles, roughly one-seventh the size of Lake Ontario.

As New Jersey's sponge, the Pinelands are filled with small streams and tributaries. All of these streams, and the larger rivers they feed, have their headwaters in the Pine Barrens, where they begin their calm, swollen meander to the ocean. The Mullica is the main river—a tea-colored, wide-bodied snake that at times looks higher than the land around it. It sways through the swampy lowlands with a barely discernible current. The Wading River and Bass River join the Mullica before it empties into Great Bay.

Route 563, especially, makes its way among these waterways for its entire forty-nine-mile stretch. North of the Mullica River, it crosses over the West Branch of the Wading River, the main interior Mullica tributary, three times. It also crosses smaller brooks—the Gates, Hospitality, and Little Hauken—along with another three unnamed streams that flow to the big river. South of the Mullica, 563 crosses Pine Creek, Landing Creek, and South Brook, also tributaries of the Mullica.

And that's just the moving water. The standing water includes acres of cranberry bogs, swamps and marshes, and clusters of small ponds and lakes, most made artificially for forges or logging operations that are now defunct (see color plate 12).

At the ocean end of 563 are the briny and saltwater marshes, and the waterways of Egg Harbor. The road crosses the Risley Channel and Shelter Island Bay as it heads south toward the Atlantic.

Route 563 may be the flattest asphalt ribbon of significant length in the state. From any point, standing in the bed of a pickup gives you a panoramic view. The short pines and trees make the horizon large in every direction—a Big Sky effect.

On the north end of 563, the highest elevation point is called Stormy Hill, a barely perceptible swell of ninety-one feet and certainly no cause for a manual transmission downshift.

On the south end, the highest point is the Margate Bridge, which spans the desolate Kiahs Island, Williams Island, and the Pork Island Wildlife Management (or hunting) area. The bridge descends to the twenty-five-mile barrier island that includes (north to south) Atlantic City, Ventnor, Margate (where the bridge lands), and Longport—which together make a packed shorefront that twinkles at night like a big-city skyline.

Its longer "500" cousin to the east, fifty-six-mile 539, is a similar road. Just as flat, just as wide open, and just as "Big Sky" in places.

Route 539 connects Hightstown to Tuckerton, cutting down through Cream Ridge and the racehorse farms of western Monmouth County and into the pinelands of Ocean as it walks a tightrope along the Burlington border.

In 1994, I did one of my all-time favorite *Star-Ledger* stories in Cream Ridge. It was filed after a day of driving grassy hills marked by miles of white wooden fences and discovering a geography—and subculture—of New Jersey I never knew existed.

The story started like this:

Imagine finding Joe DiMaggio, Ted Williams, Mickey Mantle, Hank Aaron and Willie Mays all living in the same retirement community. For harness racing fans, that's what Cream Ridge is like. This race-horse-rich area in western Monmouth County is often called "The Lexington of New Jersey."

It should be called "The Cooperstown of Harness Racing."

In an eight-mile radius within Cream Ridge, you can see some of the best standardbred racehorses that ever lived. Not just greats. The all-time greats. The legends. The cream of the riding crop.

At Walnridge Farm in Cream Ridge is Niatross, the Babe Ruth of harness racing.

Over at Perretti Farms in Cream Ridge is Matt's Scooter, who broke Niatross's one-mile speed record.

"If you call Niatross the Babe Ruth of harness racing, then Matt's Scooter is certainly the Joe DiMaggio," said Bob Marks, the marketing director at Perretti.

In the stall across from Matt's Scooter is Presidential Ball, one of only two North American pacers to win $3 million. The only other horse to do that was the now-deceased Nihilator, a son of Niatross. Matt's Scooter's father, Direct Scooter, is at Walnridge, a stablemate of Niatross.

See how it works. Great horses breed great horses . . .

What was missing from my *Star-Ledger* story, I see now, was the sense of place. This area, dead center New Jersey, is rural, but well-maintained—not quite elegant or quaint through and through like the Somerset Hills, but trimmed and orderly in a work-glove kind of way. This is not fox hunt or equestrian horse country, this is cradle-to-grave horse industry country . . . breeding, raising, training, racing, retiring. . . .

The champs in my story, put out to pasture and standing stud, spent their days roaming their large paddocks in the farms around Cream Ridge. It was a time and place that defined the Jersey harness racing industry in its heyday. The business began to slip a few years later. Some of the farms remain, some have been broken into mini-estates, some into three-acre developments. On June 7, 1999, Niatross was put down.

The nuances of the New Jersey harness industry, and the outlook for its future, are too complicated to wrestle with here, except to say the golden age may have passed.

South of the farms and the pretty little colonial-age villages of Hightstown and Allentown, 539 goes flat through over fifty thousand acres of sports paradise: the fifty-seven-hundred-acre Assunpink Wildlife Management Area just south of New Sharon; the twelve-thousand-acre Collier's Mills WMA; the twenty-four-hundred-acre Manchester WMA; the twenty-five-thousand-acre Greenwood Forest WMA next to Lebanon State Forest; the Stafford Forge WMA, nine thousand acres near the end of the road. The areas border or neighbor Lebanon State Forest, Wharton State Forest, Bass River State Forest, and the Edwin B. Forsythe National Wildlife Refuge. This, more than any other road, is a trip through New Jersey's greenway.

And at the end of 539 is Tuckerton, on the bay side of Little Egg harbor, a place every New Jerseyan should see to understand the maritime heritage and folk culture of the Jersey Shore. Long before there were hotels or boardwalks or beach tags, long before tourism became its most popular industry, the Barnegat Bay area was the stronghold of New Jersey's maritime trade and Tuckerton was its capital.

14. The Tuckerton Seaport Museum exhibit on the fall of the Tucker's Island Lighthouse, which collapsed into the ocean on October 12, 1927. *Star-Ledger* photo by Noah K. Murray.

Tuckerton was a busy port of entry during colonial times, the trade center for all southeast New Jersey at a time when there were hundreds of iron and logging operations in the pines.

Tuckerton has re-created its colonial port and made it a working historical museum with a replica of the Tucker's Island lighthouse. The forty-acre village pays homage to nearly defunct crafts and industries of the Barnegat Bay. The village has exhibits and displays on oystering and clamming, a cedar sawmill and boat building shop, and two duck-decoy carving shops. The Barnegat Bay Decoy and Baymen's Museum is now in the new village as a replica hunting shanty.

I learned about Tuckerton while doing a *Star-Ledger* story on New Jersey's Coastal Heritage Trail—the joint state and federal effort that created a network of historic and natural sites along the Atlantic Coast and Delaware Bay. I later wrote a book, based loosely on the official trail called, expectedly, *New Jersey's Coastal Heritage.* Like my experience at Cream Ridge, my first visit to Tuckerton was an eye-opener. This was another history and culture I never knew existed.

Here is how I described the Baymen's museum in that book:

> The museum recalls the days when men worked with their hands and a family could survive on what the earth gave them. If nothing else, the Baymen's Museum is a shrine to survival. And ingenuity. The collections here prove that man can always adapt to his environment. Over the centuries, settlers in the bay area perfected techniques to catch food from the waters and make salt from the earth's deposits.
>
> They developed ships that could overtake British freighters and boats that could sneak up on ducks. Over two centuries, Tuckerton men and women have proved one thing: the hands of the craftsman are the tools of an inventive mind.

Back on 563, history is not as well preserved. In fact, history has disappeared.

The northern part of the road, which begins off Route 72 just below the Lebanon State Forest in Burlington County, passes through some of those legendary Pine Barren hamlets that used to be towns but do little now but exist on maps—Hedger House, Speedwell, Hog Wallow, Jenkins, Jenkins Neck, Maxwell, Green Bank, Weekstown.

Only Chatsworth on the northern stretch of the road resembles a live, populated town, but it is one where strangers are quickly recognized.

"You're not from around here, are you?" asks a woman in Buzbys, the Chatsworth general store.

"Here meaning New Jersey?"

"No, here meaning here."

That may sum up how Pine Barrens folks see things.

Here is different from there. Here is away from it all. Here is sometimes hard to find.

I have been lost in the Pine Barrens.

That is not as dire as it sounds.

At least I had a car, and the car had gas in it.

15. The bridge at Green Bank on Route 563.
Photo by Mark Di Ionno.

It was in 1995 and I was out doing a story about New Jersey's out-of-the-way monuments for a *Star-Ledger* series I called "Oddball Attractions."

The idea of the story was to write about hidden or nearly forgotten monuments, like the Stephen Crane Wall (now torn down) on a vacant lot on Mulberry Street in Newark, the Fishermen's memorial on dead-end Missouri Avenue in Cape May, the Edison Light Bulb Tower on Christie Street in Edison, the two Alexander Hamilton busts, one in Weehawken (where Hamilton was shot by Aaron Burr) and the other overlooking the Great Falls (around which he designed Paterson, America's first industrial city), and the Greenwich Tea Party Monument on Ye Greate Street, where a group of Jerseyans burned British tea on December 22, 1774.

Two of the places on my list were the Chestnut Neck Battle Monument and the Carranza Memorial.

The Chestnut Neck monument, a fifty-foot concrete pedestal holding the figure of a patriot, is located in a small triangular park off Route 9 in Port Republic, Atlantic County. The monument marks the British effort on October 6, 1778, to rid the Mullica River area of the South Jersey privateers—ship captains contracted by Congress to pirate British cargo ships. The village of Port Republic was burned to the ground and ten vessels were destroyed. The privateers continued their assault on British merchant and supply ships, in the name of both independence and profit.

The Carranza Memorial marks the spot where Emilio Carranza, "the Lindbergh of Mexico," crashed and died while making a goodwill flight from Mexico City to New York on July 13, 1928. Carranza was a Mexican national hero and his death a Mexican national tragedy. Mexican schoolchildren raised money for the ten-foot limestone block with a carved plummeting bird. The monument was placed where he fell—in the middle of nowhere, Pine Barrens, New Jersey, U.S.A. I knew the monument was in Wharton State Forest, but I failed to realize—even after consulting a map—that Wharton is roughly the same size as Essex County.

I set out to visit both sites and on the same day, knowing they were both in the southeast quadrant of the state. I went straight down the Parkway to Port Republic, saw the Chestnut Neck Monument, then looked at a state map to find the best way to get to the Carranza Memorial. It wasn't too far from where I was—only about eighteen miles as the crow flies, inside Wharton State Forest at the end of a series of gray, unmarked lines on the map.

To stay on marked roads, I could go back up to Route 72 or down to Route 30 and take either road to Route 206 and get to Carranza from the north, but both seemed long-about.

Just then a state trooper pulled up. I told him I was trying to get to Carranza and he told me the quickest way was through Wharton. He directed me to Route 563 and told me of a turn I should make at Speedwell.

"It's a dirt road, but you'll see it . . . it's the only left you can make.

"That'll take you right there," he assured me.

So I started off, heading into unfamiliar territory—yet another geography and culture I did not know existed. I worked my way up the south bank of the Mullica along Clark's Landing Road (Route 634), eventually intersecting with 563 just as the trooper said I would.

I stayed on 563, awed by the flat beauty, lulled by the solitude. It was a weekday and there was no one on the road, or anywhere else, it seemed. I sped through the cranberry bogs on long stretches of perfectly straight road, down the center of the crew-cut alleys of pitch pines. It was early spring and the sky was cloudless and bright blue.

At what I thought was the appropriate place, I made the turn. I followed the dirt road to a fork and took what I thought was northwest, toward Carranza. It was a dead end. I doubled back and took the other

16. A straightaway
through the
Pine Barrens
on Route 563.
Photo by
Mark Di Ionno.

fork. I drove and drove, bumping down a sandy road that was hard in places and soft in others. As the road became less defined, and degenerated into a little more than tire tracks in the woods, I turned around again, and went back to 563. I took the next left, thinking maybe I hadn't gone far enough the first time, and again ended up on sandy roads of varying quality. I turned this way, then that, seeing nothing and no one to give me a clue. After another hour or so of kicking up dust, I found pavement—563. Now I was near Chatsworth, knowing I was too far north. I took 532 out of Chatsworth, trying to get to Carranza from the north. I turned in on the first dirt road, then hit a series of forks and right angle turns. All led to dead ends—except the one that brought me back to 563. In Chatsworth, I called my wife.

"I'm lost in the Pine Barrens," I said.

"You can't be too lost, you found a phone," she said, this being in the pre—affordable-cell-phone days.

Yes. But I couldn't find Carranza.

I headed back into the woods, and came back out after another hour, again on 563, this time south of Speedwell. I went back in, determined to find the monument the way I wanted—the quickest way, as the trooper said. But I was in no hurry. I was wandering. I was driving.

By now, the sun had moved down far enough in the sky to help me identify west. I kept heading toward it, angling at what I thought was north, over roads that now all looked familiar.

It was getting late, the sun was low and even the midget pines were casting shadows. Then suddenly, my dirt road turned to pavement. And there was a road sign. It said "Carranza Road." I saw a little park to my left, no more than a small clearing in the pines, and the shrine to the fallen aviator. I walked up the sand path to it, took notes, and ran my hand over the worn plummeting bird. I wondered if Carranza died on impact or if he died slowly, waiting for someone to come upon him in this God-forsaken forest.

I left the monument as alone as I had found it, and followed the paved road back to Route 206, to cars and trucks and fast food places and chain hotels. The adventure was over.

In John McPhee's wonderful book *The Pine Barrens* (Farrar, Straus, and Giroux, 1968) is a character named Fred Brown, who lived in Hog Wallow. He served as a sidekick and guide to McPhee as the author explored the sandy, unpaved roads and backwoods of the pinelands.

Each time they came upon an inhabited shack miles away from any road or neighbor, Fred Brown would say with admiration, "He got well in away from anybody."

He got well in away from anybody.

At first read, I thought it was odd, piney vernacular.

Then I slowed it down.

He got well in . . . away from anybody.

Not a bad place to be—well into the woods, away from everybody—once in a while, even if only for an afternoon.

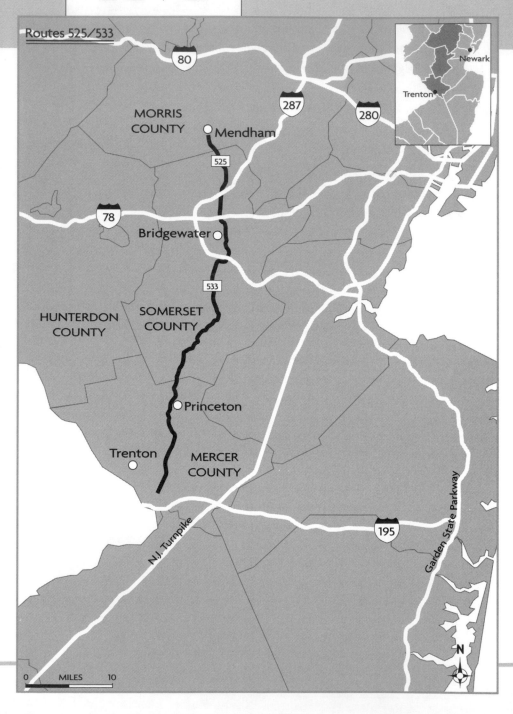

CHAPTER
FIVE

Routes 525/533

ROUTES
525
AND
533

While I was writing this book, my eighteen-year-old son, Anthony, was in a three-man alternative rock band called "Treadwell." They were good, and playing in small clubs and halls around North and Central Jersey.

One night the boys went to watch a concert at the PNC Bank Arts Center, where they were recognized by group of teenage girls.

"Aren't you the guys from Treadwell?" they asked.

The girls gushed about the boys' latest show and said they listened to all their CDs on Napster.

"It was cool to be recognized like that," my kid later said.

"I know how you feel," I said, "except that all my groupies are seventy-five-year-old men."

I never set out to be a paperback authority on the Revolutionary War in New Jersey, but I am. I know where almost every monument and marker pertaining to the war lies, whether it is imbedded in a sidewalk on an ever-widening road, or partially hidden by overgrowing brush.

I found these places for the book *A Guide to New Jersey's Revolutionary War Trail* (New Brunswick: Rutgers University Press, 2000), which was a catalog of 350 American Revolution sites statewide, far more than had ever been collected in one place. Suddenly I found myself—a third-generation Italian-American—speaking and signing books in front of the Sons of the American Revolution, the Friends of the Monmouth Battlefield, and other historical societies and groups of military history buffs.

The book was well received by history hobbyists and I was, and remain, delighted and somewhat surprised by how much it has been appreciated.

The idea for that book—like the idea for this book—started on a "500"-series road.

While deciding where to travel for my 1993 *Star-Ledger* series on the "500" roads, I took out a map of New Jersey and began tracing the longest routes, sometimes connecting two roads that would either create a loop or complete a corridor.

I picked 525 and 533 because they made a long drive (forty-nine miles) and because they would take me through familiar territory (the backroads of the Somerset Hills and greater Princeton). I also liked the way the roads visited different layers of economic and social strata. From upscale, colonial-age Mendham to struggling Manville, a town made by and named after an asbestos plant. From intellectual, separatist Princeton to industrial Finderne, the shot-and-beer section of Bridgewater that defines Chemical Work, New Jersey. From the backwater, forgotten canal village of Griggstown, to the headache-to-traverse, high-growth sections of Hamilton Township.

That's what I knew.

What I didn't know was this: the 525 and 533 corridor, connecting the Morristown area with the Trenton area, is a drive-through lesson in New Jersey's very rich Revolutionary War history.

The vestiges are everywhere. Roadside historic markers of varying vintages, worn bronze plaques inlaid in rocks and monuments are posted outside churches and houses or at places where such sites used to stand. One "Washington was here" obelisk stands like a concrete corn stalk in a farmer's field. The brown-and-white state historic-site signs pointing toward places like the Wallace House, Rockingham, and the Princeton Battlefield pop up along the road.

These roads, which form nearly a straight line down the center of the state, were well-traveled in colonial times, just as their next-door neighbor—Route 206—is today.

Yes, George Washington slept here. He also visited dying soldiers here, worshiped here, won a battle here. He set up three headquarters near here and spied on the British from here. He rode these colonial streets leading a battered army, then paraded on them to a hero's welcome at war's end.

"New Jersey has been called the Cockpit of the Revolution," said

H. Kels Swan, who owns the extensive Revolutionary War collection at Washington Crossing State Park. "Well, if New Jersey was the cockpit, this area was the center of the cockpit. There was a lot of action here."

Eighteenth-century experts like Swan estimate only 3 to 5 percent of the structures that existed at the time of the Revolution are still standing today, but along 525 and 533 there is still a lot to see. After I made that first trip, I tried to research the sites and look for added places I might have missed. I thought this would be easy. Surely somebody in Trenton had a list of all the important Revolutionary War sites. When I realized that one master list didn't exist, and that information had to be gathered county by county, town by town, historic society by historic society, I decided to collect as many as I could and write my own Rev War book.

But something else happened to me along this route one day.

I looked at myself in the rearview mirror and saw my father.

There comes a time—a moment of clarity, really—when a child has grown out of complete self-centeredness enough to understand that parents are not omnipotent after all, but filled with longing and restlessness and a desire, at times, to be something or somewhere else.

For me, this moment of clarity came at Monticello, the home of Thomas Jefferson.

My father had taken us to the Blue Ridge Mountain region on vacation, and we had just finished touring Jefferson's house and gardens. It was late in the day, and my father looked out over the Virginia Piedmont. With the sky turning pink and orange and the mountains purple in the fading light, my father seemed at ease.

"I could do this forever," he said to nobody. "I could do this every day of my life and not get bored with it."

I was maybe ten years old at the time and I knew exactly what he meant. He wanted to wander and discover.

At that moment, I felt a spiritual bond with my dad because for me, too, even as a kid, it was never just about the destination, it was also about the freedom of the ride.

At that moment, I realized we weren't at Monticello to just sightsee, or to be educated or to have our horizons broadened. We were at Monticello for the same reasons we went everywhere else. To let my father wander. To see not only Monticello, but everything between here and there. To let him breathe and shake free of the house and the job and all the other things you can escape only for precious moments when you are conditioned to be a responsible person. To free himself of the ordinary-everyday, get a ribbon of road in front of him, pull on it, and unwrap a memory.

In summers, when he was off from school, we took spur-of-the-moment rides all the time—to Spruce Run, to High Point, to the Delaware Water Gap, to Sandy Hook, to Spring Lake, to Cape May, to the Statue of Liberty, to Saratoga, to the Poconos, to Gettysburg. These were the one-day trips. Every family vacation involved the family car—for the most part a Chevy Malibu station wagon. (I have only flown on an airplane with my father once, when I took him to a Las Vegas title fight when I was a New York sportswriter. I was thirty-three at the time.)

I never remember getting restless in the car, and I never remember sleeping, either. I remember only the wind whipping around through the open windows, diluting my father's cigar smoke. I remember looking out the window, or over my father's shoulder through the windshield. I remember how liberating it was to sit in the front seat, with its unobstructed views of the world going by, like some child copilot in the cockpit. I remember the flowing, moist night air, goosebumps on sunburn.

I did this when I became a father. When my children were little, I strapped them in car seats and lulled them off to sleep in the moving car, their sweaty little heads cooled off by the rushing air, which diluted my cigarette smoke.

When they got bigger, and not as susceptible to napping, the rides to nowhere were no longer acceptable. We had to come in off the road and go *somewhere*. It was now my turn to drag my kids—often against the will of one or two—to visit places of interest. Of interest to me, at least.

Many of these trips came while I was researching one of my New Jersey books—a better cover than my father ever had to just get out and drive.

It was on this route—525 and 533—that I was hit by the cyclical reality of it all.

It was a Sunday in fall, fall being the only reliably gorgeous season we have in this state. I had five of the kids with me—the baby stayed home with her mother.

We started early, driving the route so I could take pictures for the book. Most of the route is clearly early American. You can see it in the colonial architecture, clapboard or flat stone, and the girth of the hardwood trees. You can see it in the Americana—eagles over doorways, the fife-and-drum milk cans and mail boxes, the wagon-wheel lawn ornaments. You can tell that the road is an old stage route, because it always takes the path of least resistance, winding around hills and running along rivers as it connects a series of villages older than the nation.

And so we set out to turn a few back pages of American history in what was the breadbasket of the New Jersey colony.

We walked through the cemetery at the postcard-quaint Hilltop (First Presbyterian) Church on Route 525 in Mendham, where twenty-seven Continental Army soldiers are buried. The men died at an older church on the same site, which was used as a sick bay during a Jockey Hollow smallpox epidemic. The pastor died, too, having contracted the disease from the men he cared for. Washington is said to have visited the church. It burned down in the 1800s, after lightning hit the steeple. That steeple towered over the surrounding swells of hills just as the current one-hundred-thirty-foot steeple does today.

We wound down the road through Bernardsville, whose old library building, once a colonial tavern, is said to be haunted by the ghost of a young woman still grieving for her lover, hanged as a British spy.

Further down the road, in Bridgewater, we looked out over Chimney Rock, a Watchung Mountain spy outpost for Washington. Just off 525 in Bridgewater, the kids ran through the Washington Camp Ground, where a replica of the Betsy Ross Stars and Stripes flies twenty-four hours a day. Legend has it that the new American flag flew over the heads of the Continental Army for the first time here on June 14, 1777, during the first Middlebrook encampment.

We saw historic houses off 533, where the wealthy entertained either American or British officers, depending on which army was in town.

We saw the Millstone Historic district along 533. On South River Road, little more than an alley one block east of 533, we found a plaque detailing "Simcoe's Raid" in 1779, a fifty-five-mile marauding spree by British Colonel John Simcoe and his Loyalist Queen's Rangers, who stole from Millstone valley farmers and burned down the courthouse. Two years earlier, Washington and his army had come up this road after the Battle of Princeton on their way to Morristown. Some British pursued, invaded the home of Peter Vanderveer and stole supplies. We saw that marker, too.

Using an out-of-print book, we found the home of legendary spy John Honeyman, near 533 in the Delaware and Raritan Canal village of Griggstown (see color plate 13).

We went over to nearby Rockingham, where Washington wrote his farewell orders to his officers and some of my kids played colonial games and tried on colonial costumes.

We saw the grand colonial structures of Princeton—Nassau Hall, where Congress hid, the mansions of Drumthwacket, now the state Governor's Mansion, and Morven, once owned by Richard Stockton, who signed the Declaration of Independence.

We visited the Princeton Battlefield Park just off 533, and saw the great oak (now down) where General Mercer was mortally wounded. We saw the unassuming gravesite of Richard Stockton at the Friends Meeting House around the corner.

We found a few of the Washington route markers—a couple off Route 533, one right in the middle of a cornfield.

We worked quickly. There was a lot of ground to cover and a lot of history to uncover. We stopped, took in enough to say we'd been there, and kept moving. The cataloging of these sites was a legitimate excuse to wander, to explore New Jersey's oldest cities, historic villages, and backroads.

I made many trips with my children like that as I researched my book, and it was those trips that inspired me to open the introduction like this: "I am not a historian, and this is not a book about history. This is a book about discovery."

And later on, "More than anything else . . . [this book] is a road adventure. It's a book about exploring the cities and countryside, finding the roadside markers and the forgotten plaques that tell us something happened here. Our history is out there—in our busy cities and rural towns, in our public historic sites and in private homes, in fading historical society markers and cemetery memorials."

Two scenes from that day are permanent snapshots, both in my unorganized photo stacks and in my mind's eye.

The first is of my son Matthew, then four, emerging from the cloakroom at Rockingham in a three-cornered hat and a period coat with fashionable big cuffs and tails. In terms of cuteness, it is an image for the ages.

The second is of all the kids, standing at the lookout at Washington Rock in Green Brook, on the southern ridge of the Watchungs, the big kids holding the little kids up to see. Despite the protestations of the older kids, young teens on the verge of being too cool to be seen with their camera-toting dad, the trip was working. The sites, and the scenery, were holding their interest. Now, looking down at the Raritan basin, high enough to sense the curve of the earth, high enough to pick out familiar buildings and distant bridges, to see the sparse forest of steeples and water towers, beacons of life in different towns, I wondered if they saw a world down there waiting for them. To drive and discover. To wander—like their father and grandfather—and embrace their inherent nature.

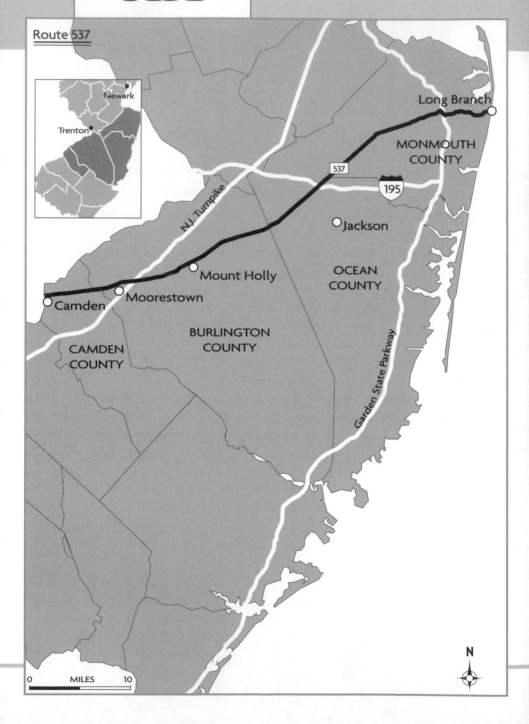

Route 537

Newark

Trenton

Long Branch

MONMOUTH
COUNTY

537

195

N.J. Turnpike

Jackson

Mount Holly

OCEAN
COUNTY

Camden

Moorestown

CAMDEN
COUNTY

BURLINGTON
COUNTY

Garden State Parkway

N

0   MILES   10

R O U T E
537

Because of New Jersey's wasp-waisted shape, the longest "500" roads run north-and-south, through the extended corridors of North and South Jersey. Only 527—which goes from the Caldwells in suburban Essex County to Toms River in Ocean County—connects north and south.

All the other "500" roads of fifty miles or more—513, 517, and 519 in the north and 553, 555, and 563 in the south—are long backroad trips through their halves of the state. These roads, all odd-numbered, take long, mostly unencumbered journeys through the distinct regions—the Highlands, the Pine Barrens, the Coastal Plain of the Delaware Bay—vast areas less populated and with more-apparent natural features than the built-up New York or Philadelphia suburbs.

The roads that run east-to-west—all even-numbered—are shorter but more compact in their scenic and demographic sweep: 510, which begins in downtown Newark and ends a world away in downtown Chester; 512, which begins in the ultra-affluent suburb of Summit and ends in one of New Jersey's extant country towns of Califon; and 514, which begins in the shadow of the monstrous and stinky Bayway refinery in industrial Linden—the source of much New Jersey Turnpike ridicule—and ends in the quiet and homey Hunterdon County village of Ringoes.

And then there is 537—the exception to the rule on many fronts.

For one, its odd-number designation makes it officially a north-south road, but geographically it runs truly more east-to-west. In fact, it is the only "500" road to cut clear across the state, going coast-to-coast. Route 537 begins one block from the Atlantic Ocean as Broadway, the main street in the reviving shore city of Long Branch, and ends on the Delaware River as Federal Street, the main street through the sadness and despair of Camden.

Route 537 is also the only road—except for 514—to join East and West Jersey. The shore area near Long Branch is clearly a New York suburb

17. A straightaway on Route 537.
Photo by Mark Di Ionno.

(with the Garden State Parkway and the Highlands ferries to the city not far away) and 537 ends in Camden five blocks from the Ben Franklin Bridge to Philadelphia.

It is also the most symmetrical road in the state. Unlike the North Jersey east-west roads that go from city (east) to country (west), or the South Jersey roads that go vice-versa, 537 starts out urban on both ends, traverses equal amounts of suburbia and exurbia on both ends, and goes through the heart of the mid-Jersey farmlands for about forty miles in the middle.

One more thing.

Roy Crazy Horse, the chief of the Powhatan Renape Indian nation off 537 in Rancocas, speaks for the whole road when he says, "We have things here [in the Rankokus Indian Reservation] you've never seen before."

The road is part exotic, part historic, and part just plain weird.

There is the Great Adventure drive-through safari trail in Jackson, with transplanted elephants, rhinos, baboons, and big cats wandering around their new environs in the Jersey Pines. There is the three-hundred-acre Indian reservation on land that used to be part of the Rancocas State Park and is open to the public.

"We have a traditional trail where people can see a traditional village with wigwams and thatched-grass long houses," Crazy Horse said. Each year, in early October and around Memorial Day, the Powhatan hosts the largest Native American arts festival on this side of the continent.

"We have . . . storytellers, wisdom keepers, alligator wrestlers. We have people come from all over to perform ceremonial dances. We have a one-hundred-foot pole that is used by the Totonaco Indians of Mexico in a ceremonial dance. They dance on the top of it, they swing off it. It's something to see. One year it was windy and I tried to keep them off there, but they wouldn't listen. They went up anyway." (There are no signs for the Rankokus reservation off Route 537, but a turn north on Rancocas Road in Mount Holly will take you there).

There is the under-glass tribute to World War II homing pigeons at the U.S. Army Communications Electronics Museum at Fort Monmouth off 537 near Eatontown. And there is the New Jersey State Aquarium, exotic in its sea-life display and weird in its location: a state with more than two hundred miles of Atlantic Ocean and Delaware Bay coastline has opted to put an aquarium on the industrial Camden waterfront.

In between, there are little things like:

— The cinder-block, freshly-painted "Joe's Peaches," which looks like a bus shelter in the middle of a cornfield near Arney's Mount Road just east of Route 206.

— The concrete animal store at Jobstown.

— The three roadside Victorian farmhouses, all deserted, separated only by narrow alleyways and surrounded by open fields.

— The gold-helmeted Mercury heads on the freshly painted, baby-blue-and-white gate to Havistock Farm. The ornate gate looks otherworldly in front of the nineteenth-century farmhouse, something like Louis XVI meets American Gothic.

— The flower farms near Sykesville (see color plate 14).

18. Havistock Farm on 537.
Photo by Mark Di Ionno.

— Soldiers in full woolen outfits battling in the stifling hot fields of Monmouth Battlefield each June.

— The New Egypt Flea Market and Farm Auction, acres and acres of little run-down junk-trading shacks that are themselves cast-offs. The buildings include a former one-room schoolhouse, a summer camp building, a miniature golf office, and old Fort Dix barracks.

— The roller coasters and Ferris wheels of Great Adventure rising suddenly out of the scrub pines of Jackson.

— Twenty-two miles of completely straight road between New Egypt and Freehold. No turns, no curves, and no hills to speak of. Automatic-pilot straight. Bonneville-Salt-Flat straight.

— The intersection of 537 and 539, which is dead center New Jersey. The true geographic center of the state is in Mercer County's Hamilton Township, five miles southeast of Trenton. But if you drew equidistant lines from High Point and Cape May and from the Atlantic to the Delaware, the place in the crosshairs would be just northwest of the intersection of 537 and 539.

19 and 20. The New Egypt Auction and Farmer's Market.
Photos by Mark Di Ionno.

And this center of New Jersey—the nation's most densely populated state—seems to be the middle of nowhere. The intersection is near Hornerstown, on the Monmouth-Ocean county border in the northeast end of the Pine Barrens. Two of the corners of this intersection are empty. On a third corner is a real-estate office in a little yellow bungalow, and on the fourth corner is a recreational vehicle dealership. This intersection hasn't changed much since I wrote the "500" road series for the *Star-Ledger*. There is a new traffic light, and the RV place, which was then a fledgling business, has more rolling homes on its lot.

"It only seems like it's in the middle of nowhere," Jim Germaine of the RV dealership told me. "You'd be surprised how much traffic we get. It's quite a busy intersection."

That's true. Cars, which materialize from nothing and seem to be going nowhere, don't exactly clog the intersection, but appear with some regularity. But down the road each way, except for a small farm stand and a cluster of three prefab ranches on 539, there is nothing but woods.

Also true is this: the intersection is only minutes from heavily developed areas. Going east, it's five minutes from Great Adventure, twenty minutes from Freehold, thirty-five minutes from Long Branch through the pleasant horse-and-landed-gentry country of Colts Neck.

South of the four corners, Tuckerton is thirty-five minutes away and Long Beach Island forty-five. North of the intersection are Allentown (fifteen minutes) and entrances to Interstate 195 and the Turnpike. West, Mount Holly is half an hour, and Moorestown, the Short Hills of South Jersey, is fifty minutes.

The point of all this is to illustrate two things: First, the state is so compact through the middle, everything is close. Second, the state is not as overcrowded and hopelessly overdeveloped as we sometimes think, because at this junction—reasonable commuting distance from New York, Newark, Philadelphia, and Trenton—you get a woodsy sense of isolation. These are backroads, not inhabited by cosmopolitan people (we think). And yet they are closer to Philadelphia than people in Morristown are to New York.

Development has come slow to this bull's-eye interior for a number of reasons, but mostly because it is equidistant from the traditional population centers and the creeping growth from northeast and southwest just hasn't got there yet. When it does, it will have to sidestep the twenty-mile contiguous swath of U.S. military installations of McGuire–Fort Dix–Lakehurst and the twelve-thousand-acre Collier's Mills Wildlife Management Area, which is the northern extension of Lebanon State Forest. It will have to sidestep the federal and state building restrictions on these parts of the Pinelands. And it will have to sidestep people like Rich Walling and the Friends of Monmouth Battlefield, who are securing lands around the state park, preserving them for historical posterity.

Some areas around the Monmouth Battlefield look much as they did on that searing hot day of June 28, 1778, when American forces attacked the back end of a twelve-mile-long, fifteen-hundred-wagon British Army train on its way to Sandy Hook. Before it was over, it became the longest battle of the Revolution and the battle involving the most troops. It was a battle that gave birth to an American heroine, that solidified George Washington's reputation as a field leader, and elevated the status of the American army from amateur to professional (see color plate 15).

The battle covered about a fifteen-mile span, but the main site, or "killing fields," as state historian Garry Wheeler Stone says, was the soft hills and meadows between Tennent and what today is Freehold, where the state park is.

The battle took place on a typical mid-Jersey summer day: brutally hot, thickly humid, with no breeze to circulate the sticky air. The kind of day when the call of the cicadas crackles through the air like radio static and the heat lightning shocks the evening sky but fails to deliver its electric promise of a cooling rain.

In the early morning hours, American General Charles Lee advanced with his force of five thousand men to attack the rear guard of the British procession. Lee was supposed to stand and fight, to give Washington a chance to move in with his force of eight thousand. But when Lee realized he was up against much more than the rear guard, he fell back in a panicked retreat, crossing the path of Washington in full advance mode.

Washington intercepted Lee and demanded he turn and fight. When Lee balked, Washington exploded.

Washington unleashed years of pent-up anger at his long-time antagonist, calling him a "damned poltroon," challenged his courage and loyalty, and ordered him to the rear. General Charles Scott, a witness to the incident, said Washington "swore . . . till the leaves shook on the trees." Washington took charge, rode through the lines and rallied the men. Sometime during the battle, Molly Hays, who was bringing water to the exhausted troops, took over the cannon duty of her injured husband and the legend of Molly Pitcher was born. Washington's leadership and Molly Pitcher's heroism are only part of the story.

Perhaps the most important part is the Americans' newfound ability to stand and fight in open warfare. Drilled by Baron von Steuben at Valley Forge, the Continental Army raised its standards of engagement in Monmouth, going from a ragtag bunch of farmers with muskets to a well-trained army.

In *A Guide to New Jersey's Revolutionary War Trail*, I wrote:

There is no better illustration of this than the death of [British] Lieutenant Henry Monckton, who was in command of the redcoat elite troops. Three times they charged an American line commanded by "Mad" Anthony Wayne. Each time, Wayne had his men stand their ground. The last time, he let the British advance so close that he and Monckton could hear one another's orders.

"Forward to the charge, my brave grenadiers," Monckton is said to have ordered as he led a full-speed charge.

"Steady . . . steady," Wayne told his troops. "Wait for the word, then pick out the kingbirds."

When the British came within forty yards, Wayne ordered his troops to fire. The British charge disintegrated into a heap of falling men, one of whom was Monckton. He was so close that some of the Americans went out and seized his sword and colors, the trophies of war.

Monckton is buried at Tennent Church, just off the west side of the state park.

I have spent many days at Monmouth Battlefield, usually around the time of the rollicking annual reenactment, which is part history lesson, part theater, and part fireworks. Thousands of spectators come out to see hundreds of reenactors, clothed in the heavy woolen outfits of the period despite the usually ninety-degree late-June temperatures, march through the fields, imitating the movements of the forces in the actual battle, blasting cannons and firing musket fusillades at each other. (Funny how they all die in the shade.)

Monmouth Battlefield is otherwise a quiet park. It is one of the few unspoiled American Revolution battlefield sites in the country, and there are plans underway to restore the eighteenth-century plant life and natural vegetation to complete its authenticity. From the ridge behind the interpretive center, above the battlefield, you see nothing but trees, shrubbery, and grassy fields, deer grazing in the meadow and birds arching through the air. The only signs of humanity are the rough cross-picket fences that line the fields and the occasional hiker or dog-walker on the battlefield trail.

I remember one summer trip there, with a bunch of extended family members. We let the kids run out and shatter the silence of the hot, humidity-muted fields.

One of my cousins—who lives in Colts Neck and has watched the area change from pastoral horse country to the land of ostentatious mini-estates over the last two decades—said to the kids, "There was a time when all of New Jersey looked like this."

True enough.

Truer still, much of it still does. You just have to know where to look.

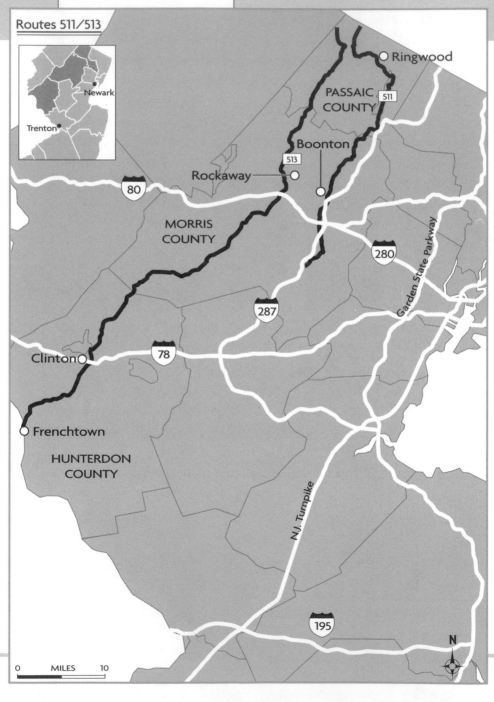

CHAPTER
SEVEN

Routes 511/513

Newark

Trenton

O Ringwood

PASSAIC
COUNTY

511

Boonton

513

Rockaway

80

MORRIS
COUNTY

280

Garden State Parkway

287

ClintonO

78

O Frenchtown

HUNTERDON
COUNTY

N.J. Turnpike

195

N

0   MILES   10

The rugged, pock-marked lake country of northern Morris and Passaic counties is today considered either suburban or rural, and the roads that run through it—Routes 511 and 513— climb rocky hills, dip sharply into Highlands valleys, and skirt placid lakes and large reservoirs surrounded by hardwood forests.

It's hard to believe this was once an industrial area.

The iron ore in these hills, along with the cooling rivers tumbling down through the mountains, made this part of New Jersey perfect for iron foundries in the eighteenth and nineteenth centuries.

The same geographic characteristics that spawned the iron industry in New Jersey have also made the Highlands lake region the drinking water-supply base for most of urban New Jersey. When iron went out, reservoirs came in, as the fast-moving streams and rivers of the area were dammed, creating giant basins of water in low-lying areas.

Both 511 and 513 share this history. In fact, both roads pretty much began as iron ore transport routes, linking the forge towns along the way. There were forges on the Whippany River in Hanover (511), Morristown (511), and Dover (513) and along the Rockaway River in Boonton (511) and Hibernia (513). The names of towns along 513—Ironia, Succasunna (Suckysunny was the Lenape name for iron ore), Mine Hill— reflect the iron history (see color plate 16).

The mines and forges played an important role in America's early wars.

The Ford-Faesch iron works in Mount Hope and Hibernia (today part of Rockaway Township on 513) was the leading supplier of arms, ammunition, and tools to the Continental Army during the American Revolution. The hundred or so forges in the Morris County area were one reason Washington stayed close to Morristown for much of the eight-year war. He knew the iron in the hills could keep his soldiers armed.

Up in Passaic County, Ringwood (off 511) was king. Iron pulled out of about twenty mines in the Ramapo Mountains was forged at Long Pond (511), Pompton, Charlotteburg (off Route 23), and Newfoundland (513). Robert Erskine, the ironmaster at Ringwood during the Revolution, became a confidant of Washington's and made over two hundred local maps for the general while the smiths at his forge hammered out munitions.

Over in Boonton, the iron works made most of the cannons and cannonballs for the Union Army during the Civil War.

The Ford-Faesch operation was just over Green Pond Mountain from what today is the U.S. Army's high-tech modern arsenal at Picatinny. Picatinny, a weapons development facility established in 1880 by the U.S. War Department, is in fact the great-grandson of Ford-Faesch, which was the first in a long gray line of munitions-related industries on the mountain.

During its heyday Hibernia was the biggest town in Morris County. Dover, Boonton, Wharton, and Rockaway all thrived with the building of the Morris Canal. The ore and goods were transported by mule-pulled barges on hand-dug waterways from the interior to the port areas east. As many as fifty mines were operating between Long Valley and Hibernia during the 1800s.

The industry knew no loyalty. Boonton was a leading maker of train car wheels and axles and steel rails—supplying the booming railroad industry with the weapons to kill the canals.

Millions of tons of ore were taken out of the New Jersey Highlands during the 1700s and 1800s, and the mineshafts grew deeper and the process became more expensive in the continuous search for more reserves. Mine bosses went looking for more fertile fields, and found them near Lake Superior in the early 1880s. Within twenty years, the iron industry in New Jersey was dead, and the forge villages became ghost towns.

21. The Monksville Reservoir on Route 511.
Photo by Mark Di Ionno.

Long Pond Ironworks on 511 was one of those places, and for years the buildings along the Monksville Reservoir stood empty, neglected reminders of a forgotten past.

I found Long Pond for the first time on a beautiful fall day, when the oak and maple leaves of the hardwood forest were ablaze against the bright blue skies and deep green waters of the reservoir. I pulled into the deserted village and walked back into the woods along a wide path. I found the stone ruins and overgrown foundations of other buildings, and a number of clapboard structures still standing but ready to fall. I wanted to know more about the mysterious place. On my next trip back, I found a man working. His name was Martin Deeks, and he was the vice president of a group called the Friends of Long Pond.

"We're here because this was an important place and we don't want it to be forgotten," Deeks told me. "We all have homes that need the grass cut, or need minor repairs, and some of our wives don't understand why we spend so much time here. They say, 'Nothing will ever come of that place.'"

Deeks said Long Pond is unique in that "it may be the only place in the country where a furnace and hydro-power system from colonial times and one from the Civil War era stand side by side. Usually, they tore down the old furnace, before building a new one."

In the six years since, the Friends of Long Pond have made great progress, rehabbing some of the old buildings as they try to get a Waterloo-type village up and running.

"Our long-range plan is for the restoration of at least eight of the buildings, creating a whole museum village," Deeks said. "We could adapt some of the old buildings to new uses—like a gift shop. The workers' houses could be restored to what they once were, complete with working-class furnishings of the day, which would be a nice contrast to what people see at Ringwood." (Ringwood Manor, the home of the iron-masters of the Ringwood works, is a richly appointed tourist site owned and operated by the state.)

Before its demise, Long Pond was home to about one hundred workers and their families. They lived in company housing, shopped in company stores, and went to company schools. The village at Long Pond was more like a plantation than a company town. There were small farms to keep the village supplied with dairy products, grain, fruits, vegetables, and meat. A sawmill kept the village builders flush in lumber. A blacksmith shop shoed and harnessed the mules and oxen used to haul iron, and kept the wagons in good repair. In all, it was a self-sufficient little community. A church, built in the town's later years, still stands.

With iron out, water became the most important natural resource in the Highlands region of 511 and 513.

Route 511 runs past two giant reservoirs—the Jersey City Reservoir in Boonton, which holds about eight billion gallons of water, and the Wanaque Reservoir, a six-mile-long basin that holds thirty billion, and a few smaller reservoirs including scenic Taylortown (see color plate 17).

Route 511 crosses the Jersey City Reservoir between Boonton and Parsippany, over the oldest steel bridge in Morris County. The sun and moon both rise over the water to the east, luminous balls mirrored in the sheen of the lake. As you turn down 511 toward the reservoir, and the road dips to meet the bridge, you get a sudden sense of being someplace else—like the upper peninsula of Michigan or the Adirondack lake region of New

York State—someplace where the little forested island in the middle of the reservoir belongs. A someplace painted by a landscape artist in the wild. A place not Boonton, New Jersey, two miles from the busy junction of Interstates 80 and 287.

The same is true of the Wanaque Reservoir. It goes on for miles, a long pond at the base of a cluster of high rounded hills. It is a simply beautiful backdrop, something you would expect to see in the Pacific Northwest or the Thousand Lakes region of Canada. For some of this drive you are right up against the water, crossing bridges that separate coves from the main lake. In summer, the hills are green and sunlight glistens off the blue water. In winter, the wind howls off the hills and the water turns four shades darker than the gray February skies. At the Monksville Dam, a large concrete bunker just off 511, you feel that wind in every season, blowing down from New York State across the long prairie of reservoir. You can walk across the dam, braced against that wind, and again get a sense of being somewhere else, somewhere remote, somewhere wild.

Route 513—all eighty-five miles from where it starts in Frenchtown to where it ends in Upper Greenwood Lake, north of West Milford—is filled with such scenery.

Like neighboring 519, the southern part of 513 connects a series of country towns in Hunterdon County, postcard rural hamlets like French-town, Pittstown, Clinton, and High Bridge.

The road begins in Frenchtown—a smaller and less commercial version of Lambertville—an undiscovered walk-around town of antique shops and artist's studios. Frenchtown sits on the banks of the Delaware, with a riverside park and restaurants overlooking the Uhlerstown-Frenchtown Bridge. A decade ago, the drafty studios of the Gem Building were filled with struggling craftspeople and artists. (I interviewed a woman there once who was a tapestry maker.) But in the past few years, some of these folks have moved out, giving way to more successful, slicker artisans.

Up the road from Frenchtown is Pittstown, a small enclave of 1700s stone structures that, like those in Hope on 521, have been restored as

22. Fairmount Church
at 512 and 513.
Photo by Mark Di Ionno.

real-estate offices and restaurants. The road continues through the
pleasant rolling hills of Hunterdon and down into Clinton.

Clinton was a country town. Now, like Chester on 510, it is a *faux*
country town. The mills—yes, the famous Red Mill—are art galleries and
antique shops. The downtown shops are all specialty restaurants or craft
stores. The people are all from out of town. Only the ones wading in the
South Branch of the Raritan, fly-fishing for trout beneath the falls, seem
to be authentic Clintonites.

From Clinton, 513 begins climbing the south slope of the Musconetcong Mountains, winding through High Bridge and up to Voorhees State

Park. In Voorhees is a scenic overlook of the South Branch valley below. The park also has the Paul Robinson Observatory, from which you can view the sights above. North of Califon, 513 splits a pair of mountain ridges through the aptly named Middle Valley section, a fertile section of Washington Township. There the remaining nurseries and produce farms take advantage of the dark, nutritious soil, just as miners once tapped into the rocks for the black ore (see color plate 18).

Through here, 513 is largely agricultural, but it is changing to suburbia. Long Valley is clogged with traffic, and the road, as it heads toward Chester and Randolph, becomes congested during peak hours.

It is only after you go through Rockaway that 513 returns to its natural state—an old mine road cutting through the jagged hills that gave an iron industry to a fledgling nation.

That industry is gone now, its building foundations left to disintegrate in the woods, and miles of mines boarded up, overgrown, or filled in, the old towns and their stories receding into history, remembered only in dusty library books and the occasional rusted roadside marker.

And at least one of its caves has gone to the bats.

At the Wildcat Ridge Wildlife Management Area, there is a platform overlooking an abandoned Hibernia mine that has attracted millions of bats. In late summer and early fall, they can be seen moving like a giant cloud out of the cave at sunset, a black mist that dissipates into the night. They fly through the mountainside, feeding and mating, a swarm of a colony living a nocturnal life, spending daylight in the cold, dark mine.

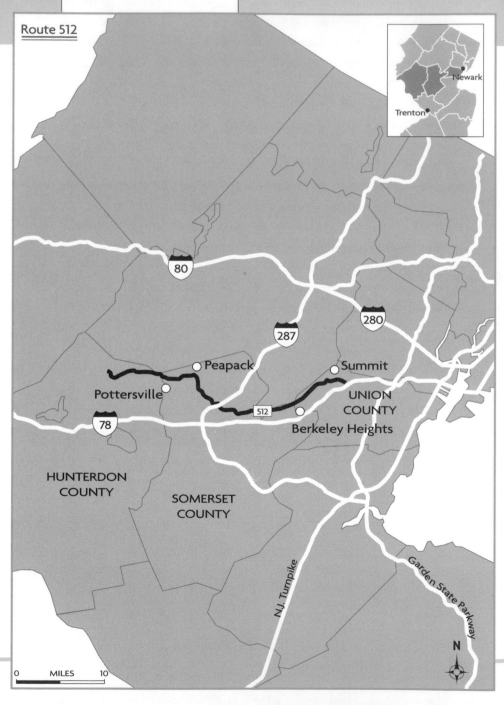

Route 512

Newark

Trenton

80

280

287

512

Peapack

Summit

Pottersville

UNION
COUNTY

78

Berkeley Heights

HUNTERDON
COUNTY

SOMERSET
COUNTY

N.J. Turnpike

Garden State Parkway

N

0   MILES   10

ROUTE
512

I stood outside the fly-fishing shop of Les Shannon in downtown Califon, just a block from the bridge that spans the South Branch of the Raritan (see color plate 19). It was one of those sun-warmed days, late in March on the winter-spring cusp, about a week or two before the opening of a new trout season.

Les is a master fly-tier. From bits of feather, fuzzy stuff, and special string he can craft a phony insect realistic enough to fool a trout into thinking dinner is skipping along the stream surface. He spent hours with me explaining the rudiments of fly-tying for a *Star-Ledger* story, then we drove to the thaw-swollen Ken Lockwood Gorge, a beautiful and popular spot for those in the cult of trout fishing. Now Les was giving me "quickest way" directions to get me back to Route 78 and the newspaper.

" . . . or you can take 512 all the way back to Route 78 in Summit," he said, pointing east on the road that ran up the hill past his shop and into the New Jersey countryside.

Somewhere in the back of my mind, I knew that.

Somewhere back in time, I had made that trip many times, pointing my box of a four-cylinder economy car west and driving out of my suburban town and into the country.

So I took the long way home, watching from west to east as the New Jersey landscape changed. On 512 the rural-mountain Hunterdon County geography outside Califon, where the Fox Hill Range reaches elevations of over one thousand feet and where the road dips down over the capillaries of mountain creeks that tumble into the South Branch, becomes rural-hilly farmland. Idyllic Pottersville is a picturesque nineteenth-century village along the Black River where Hunterdon topography meets the Somerset Hills and the well-maintained farms and in-town Victorians hold suburban sprawl at bay. In the semirural small town of Peapack-

23. A winter's day in Pottersville.
Star-Ledger photo by Aris Economopoulos.

Gladstone, with its end-of-the-line rail station and ever-growing affluence, law offices and midscale restaurants occupy restored barns, mills, and general stores. From there the road passes through the estate country of the Somerset Hills and the growing suburban small towns of Gillette and Stirling, where strip malls keep replacing garden centers. It ends in the well-entrenched and stable suburban town of Summit (see color plate 20).

It was during that particular drive—a rediscovery of an old carefree highway—that I got the idea for the 1993 newspaper series about the state's "500"-series roads. That series was based on things I saw—an old church here, a historic site there, nature running its course along the winding roads of the New Jersey interior.

But it was my visceral attachment to 512, and that day's fifty-miles-per-hour scenery sweep of memory and emotion through my own back-roads, that gave me the idea for this book.

Route 512, you see, begins where I do, in East Summit.

I was a toddler in 1957 when my family moved from the Shore into a three-bedroom, post–World War II Cape on Edison Drive, a kid-filled neighborhood just up the hill from a woodsy place called Briant Park. Briant Pond, on land once owned by colonial Summit-settler Cornelius Briant, is where I learned to ice-skate on double blades. The woods I later explored behind the pond led to the Houdaille quarry, one of many traprock operations in the Watchung Mountains; some of the dug-out cliffs there looked Grand Canyonesque to a six-year-old. I would learn later on that George Washington was in the area during the Battle of Springfield, perhaps staying at Jacob Bryant's Tavern at what today is the Broad Street interchange of Route 24. (There is no explanation for the spelling change of the family name.)

East Summit in those days was mostly Italian-American, and it still is to some extent. Some of the mainstays, like Natale's Bakery, are still there. When I was growing up, there were plenty of kids whose grand-parents—and sometimes parents—had heavy Italian accents. This sec-tion, on both sides of Morris Avenue and between Morris and Park Avenue, had homes with carpet-like manicured lawns, concrete patios and walkways, grape arbors and gardens in the backyards. It was the biggest contiguous area of middle-class homes in town.

That was the East Summit of the postwar building boom.

In even older days, Briant Pond was also called Spring Lake (not to be confused with the seaside resort where I happened to be born).

Summit's Spring Lake was a mountain resort in the 1880s, when the town was filled with the great estates of the Victorian-era business class. The Spring Lake Hotel, like the other Summit hotels, catered to the mem-bers of that class and those who wanted to be like them. The lake was a mountain retreat in a country setting, and for his guests' entertainment proprietor John B. McGrath formed a baseball team called the Red Stockings, who played on a field across from the hotel, where there is a car wash today.

When I was growing up—and until the time I had my first legal drink at age eighteen—the Spring Lake Tavern was the shot-and-beer place of neighborhood men, many of whom wore the forest green uniforms of city workers. The bar was dark and the house around it rundown. But like many places in this book, the tavern has come around on the cycle of time. It is now the Huntley Tavern, a refurbished and decidedly upper-midscale restaurant, although its retro Victorian porch still overlooks the car wash.

Some social critics may say it's inauthentic, a facsimile of what once was. All along 512—and many other roads in this book—you see such things: old general stores turned into bistros; old corner drugstores turned into exotic coffee shops; old grist mills turned into craft shops or art galleries; old theaters turned into exclusive indoor malls; old farms turned into housing developments with country-sounding names like Fox Run; old country towns turned into day-trip destinations for the coffee-and-craft suburban crowd. But these conversions don't make these places worse, just different. Yes, the suburbs are sprawling and, yes, the wealth belt is spreading, but history is still around.

The Summit I grew up in has changed and it hasn't: there are condominiums where the greenhouses of Caporaso's Florists used to be, and there are town houses in the woods leading up to them. But my friend Eddie Spallone's parents still live in the same house on Edison Drive they've been in for fifty-some years, and Eddie lives just a couple of blocks away. Before we know it, Eddie Spallone's kids will be celebrating their family's centennial in Summit, if they think about it.

Gus's Luncheonette, the downtown counter where I worked as a kid for emphysemic old Augie who coughed it up in the kitchen, is gone, replaced by a gourmet Asian restaurant. But Harquail Brothers, the automotive store next to Gus's, is still there. My good-looking, happy-go-lucky, hard-living Uncle Angelo worked at Harquail's and ate lunch every day at Gus's.

The history lives in the stores and homes and in the people.

So this is my history. My time, my town, my 512, which in Summit is called Springfield Avenue, the main street of the business district. I worked on the street throughout my teenage years. I quit Gus and went to work at the Kress's Five and Ten up the street, which also had a lunch counter and paid minimum wage. Kress's is now the Beacon Hill Clearview Multiplex, which replaced the aged twelve-hundred-seat Strand Theater down the street. I saw the first few hundred movies of my life at the Strand, which in those days opened with a noon show and closed when the last movie got out at midnight.

When I went to work full-time in a private market as a delivery boy after high school, I realized the town was full of guys like Gus and my Uncle Angelo. These were the townies, that mildly subversive service class in an affluent town like Summit. Some of them lived on the edge of town in giant Victorian rooming houses, like Willie, the market's produce guy, who was a divorced father of six and an art school graduate with the face of a contender, or the limping, tattooed Troast Bakery baker with the southern accent who somehow ended up here, as good a place as any.

The downtown was filled with characters, people who grew to either like or hate each other, all on a first-name-only basis, all based on what they saw of each other during the course of an eight-hour workday. It was all like scenes from a Bernard Malamud story, at least to me. I learned something that would serve me well later as an editor and writer: Every town, no matter how it appears on the surface, is filled with little tensions and subcultures and social strata clumsily bumping into each other, all worth exploring.

Like this:

When I was a grocery boy, I became, overnight, a townie. Even though I had grown up in town and gone to school with the children of some of my customers, being a townie gave me a new access to people's lives and at the same time an anonymity that kept me separated from them. I saw friends' mothers (or their neighbors) in their nightclothes and slips, in their kitchens unprepared for the world. I overheard intimate family dynamics discussed with friends in kitchens or over phones. It didn't matter. I didn't matter. I was now part of the service class, invisible, my silence (they thought) bought with a buck tip. One day while walking on Springfield Avenue, I passed a woman I delivered to three times a week, a woman who was always friendly and talkative and a good tipper.

"Hi, Mrs. Walker," I said.

She looked at me, confused, trying to place me. Who was I?

It finally came to her—and it hit me: I was a townie, trusted enough to enter her house without knocking by the kitchen door, to be alone with her in her kitchen while she at times was not completely dressed, but not important enough to be recognized on the street when detached from my Summit Food Market truck.

So, you ask, what does this have to do with "Backroads, New Jersey?"

Everything. The backroads are filled with these stories, the characters, the small-town dramas, the lives lived.

I don't know them all. Just mine. And Route 512 in Summit winds out as the main drag in my life. My younger brother was nearly killed on it, broadsided in his car by a speeding tanker truck at dawn. This was at the very corner we crossed walking to high school, just a few yards away from the spooky cloistered nunnery, which is still there with the ten-foot privacy walls we tried to peek over as kids. On the corner was the Summit Hotel (now named the Summit Grand), where I met girlfriends and, like thousands before me, tore up the clean-sheeted beds (downstairs in the hotel bar an early girlfriend's drunk father looked me in the eye once and said, "I don't like you . . . you look sneaky"—something I thought about each time I met her in the rooms above).

Around the corner were the Locust Gardens apartments. Many things happened at those apartments. When I was ten, a neatly dressed, blue-haired lady in a maroon '65 Lincoln called me "a guinea" as I walked to church. Another day a delivery van hit me on my bike as it backed out of the driveway, and I walked away with nothing more than a scraped knee and a bent front rim. We walked over the long garage roofs behind those apartments on our way to Catholic school; we could look into the back of a mental hospital. One day we saw a girl struggling under the weight of a big guy dressed in white and we yelled and threw rocks at him and he got up and chased us and called us dirty names and hopefully she got away. And I used to deliver a six-pack of Canada Dry Ginger Ale, a nine-pack of Hershey's chocolate bars, and a loaf of Pepperidge Farm bread almost every day to an old lady named Mrs. Harvey, who fell a lot and came to the door bruised and one day didn't come at all.

Down the street was the Brough funeral home, where we sent off my grandfather when I was thirteen and my grandmother thirty-one years later. All this was within a block of 512, the road I used to drive out of town.

That was my Summit.

Almost everyone else's Summit is an elegant suburb, one of the best the state has to offer.

It is the Summit where the Strand is now an upscale indoor mall, with stores with names like "Persnickety." It's the Summit where the old Fanny Farmer chocolate shop on 512 became a gourmet coffee cafe which, in turn, was run out of business when a Starbucks opened up in what had been "Cats"—an old newspaper, cigar, candy, and dirty magazine store across from the train station. The old Fanny Farmer is now a polished little restaurant called A. J.'s American Luncheonette, which clearly is no Gus's. As I said before, that doesn't make it better or worse. Just different.

Summit, the high-end suburb, begins the other side of the tracks (yes, it's true) from East Summit, just past the NJ Transit railroad trestle (it sounded so much more like a real railroad when it was called the Erie Lackawanna) as 512 climbs up the steep eastern face of the Second Watchung Mountain. From just above the trestle a panoramic and unobstructed view of the Newark Basin and the New York City skyline emerges, and many homes on the ridge have that view.

In the mid-1960s, an imposing edifice appeared on that horizon. The Twin Towers of the World Trade Center usurped the Empire State Building as a new focal point on the skyline. In Summit, the Towers' presence was more than a residential real-estate selling point. The train line to Hoboken and PATH to the World Trade Center was about a forty-minute commute on the express, making Summit one of the closest desirable suburbs in the metro region for the financial set. Summit, always rich, blossomed more. No matter which way the economy went, Summit seemed insulated because even in bad times, someone in the financial district makes money.

This aura of invincibility was shaken with the terror attack of September 11, 2001, which claimed the lives of nine Summit residents—nine people who left for work on that day as on every other. In truth, the number killed was surprisingly low, considering the number of Summit people who travel there each day. Still, Summit was as much a domestic Ground Zero as any other New Jersey place, and the town shuddered. The day of the attack, teary people gathered on high, clear points in neighborhoods throughout Summit to first watch the towers burn, then see smoke rise from where the towers had stood, and then wonder who would not be coming home that night. A week after the attack, a prayer vigil at the Village Green drew five thousand people, and a message from President George W. Bush was read by a local minister.

Summit, then, picked up where it left off, remaining the executive town in the grand Suburban Essex tradition (even though Summit is in Union County). This is the Summit which once billed itself "The City of Beautiful Homes," the Summit of fortress-like English and Normandy Tudors, of the ornate, turreted Queen Anne Victorians and the geometrical Stick and Shingle Victorians, of Gothic and Greek Revival and Italianate and Mission-style mansions. It is the Summit of the Fortnightly Club, a century-old cultural and social club for women housed in a Neoclassical mansion that is listed on the State and National Registers of Historic Places as Twin Maples, circa 1908.

It is the Summit built first as a mountain resort, then as a place for the expansive estates of the privileged few, then as home to the New York executive class. Its geography made it a pleasant place for summer retreats for the wealthy, and the Morris and Essex Railroad (through the Oranges and Summit, and on to Morristown), which first ran as early as

1837, made it convenient for New York businesspeople and their crowd. Eventually the Gladstone line was built, connecting New York with the Bernardsville area, and both lines merged in Summit. (Route 512, by the way, basically parallels the Gladstone line.)

The Summit of the old days was a town of two classes: the very rich and the people who serviced them. The ever-improving train service in the later 1800s and early 1900s brought in legions of the nearly rich—workaday executives who could afford sizable homes and comfortable lifestyles, but could not employ staffs larger than their own families. Summit through these years became a solidly upper-middle-class town, and that affluence still shows—in the homes and downtown.

The Summit of the presprawl days was on the western fringe of true suburbia. The towns west on 512—New Providence, Berkeley Heights, Gillette, Millington, Stirling—were all smaller and more countrified. While 512 was "main street" in these towns, those towns did not have the same downtown heft and old suburban feel of Summit. While not exactly rural, these towns west of Summit still had working farms on 512 in my lifetime. Most of those farms are gone, although a few farmstands, greenhouses, and nurseries are still there.

Like many towns along this west-of-Summit stretch of road, many different generations of New Providence come together in short spans.

Down the street from the First Presbyterian Church, where enough Continental Army veterans are buried for the cemetery to have earned DAR status, are two original saltbox homes from colonial days. One is a private home and one is a museum. Behind the saltbox museum is an old United Methodist Church whose cemetery is filled with peeling sandstone markers. The bell tolls for wood frame and clapboard architecture—in the background are a modern, octagonal Roman Catholic church of cedar beams and glass and a squat brick high school, very functional-industrial—both built in the last forty years.

At the Berkeley Heights–New Providence border is the first sign of the high density housing that has reshaped suburban New Jersey in the past twenty-five years. Berkeley Housing is a townhouse complex with a power line right-of-way running through it.

Berkeley Heights also has more Main Street strip mall development than either Summit or New Providence, evidence of farmland sold to developers in one chunk rather than of a gradual expansion of the downtown. In this way, Berkeley Heights has a little of both: a family-owned Italian joint just down the street from a Pizza Hut, a local pharmacy going head-to-head with Drug Fair.

The road name changes from Springfield Avenue to Valley Road in Gillette and Stirling (Long Hill Township). Stirling is named after Lord Stirling, the eccentric Revolutionary War patriot whose estate was in the area, and the road intersects in Bernards Township with King George Road, named for the villain of the era. The colonial era exists in more than the vernacular. Where 512 turns toward the Veterans' Administration hospital complex, there is a circa-1764 flat-rock-and-mortar house, still used as a private home.

The veterans' hospital at Lyons is a sprawling, WPA-era institution which was built to house the "Section 8's"—those discharged from the military for psychiatric reasons. It was not uncommon for people to walk off the grounds and hitchhike out on 512 in their blue hospital pajamas and robes, and I can remember a number of traffic fatalities involving patients from the VA hospital. The hospital is in a tranquil setting on a landscaped Somerset hillside with a nine-hole golf course out front. I remember seeing patients milling around the grounds, sitting on benches along driveways leading to blocklike sand-colored buildings. There were no gates to keep them in or you out. Clearly it was place both easy and impossible to escape from.

When I was a navy corpsman, we transported patients to Lyons now and then. I remember talking about the place with my lieutenant, a Jersey guy who had been to Vietnam, worked at the Pentagon, and gone through the military's war college. He told me that on strategic air maps, the VA hospital was listed as Bell Labs in Murray Hill and vice versa. With similar-sized campuses just a few miles apart, the government had found a decoy for one of the nation's technological nerve centers.

Beyond the VA, Route 512 cuts through Liberty Corner, a Rockwellian collection of nineteenth-century houses, a firehouse, a cluster of stores, and a grammar school, which maintains its small-town feel. It is the first of a series of small towns along 512 that make you think you're somewhere not thirty-five miles from New York.

The road continues west here through some of the most desirable and pretty real estate in all of New Jersey. This is the southeast end of the Somerset Hills, estate country—how the other one-tenth of 1 percent lives.

The rolling hills, open fields, and country club–sized mansions make it the perfect place for the United States Golf Association Museum and Library. The "Golf House" is a Georgian Colonial designed by John Russell Pope and built in 1919 as a private home. The USGA opened its museum there in 1934. The collection is typical sports Hall-of-Fame fare—clubs and equipment used by champions, a trophy room, antiques and paper memorabilia, historical and technical exhibits.

Next, hard by the Moggy Brook, comes the Leonard J. Buck Gardens, a thirty-three-acre refuge strewn with rocks left over from the rapid retreat of the Wisconsin glaciers some fifteen thousand years ago. Buck, a mining engineer, built impressive and artistic rock gardens from the prehistoric debris.

Around the bend from the Buck Gardens are the large rock walls and rock entranceways of the former Schley estate, part of which is now Moorland Farms, home of the annual steeplechase and the Midland Run.

Grant Schley, born in 1845, was a New York State farm boy who ended up working for George F. Baker, the director of American Express and president of First National Bank of New York. He moved up well in the company and married Baker's daughter. He started several other businesses and by the 1880s had amassed a fortune. In 1887 the Schleys came to this area by wagon to look at some land, fell in love with the Somerset Hills, and bought fifteen hundred acres.

The Schleys built a stone mansion, called "Froh Heim," German for happy home. Who could be sad with Schley money? The mansion was filled with exotic artifacts and antiques, including a full-size teepee in an "Indian room," and one room filled with nothing but sixty silver wasps' nests hanging from the ceiling. When the Schleys' collection

24. A concrete Japanese lantern from the old Schley estate.
Photo by Mark Di Ionno.

grew to contain too much stuff, they just added another room to the
mansion. The estate included an indoor tennis court, a swimming pool,
a stable, a horserace track, and six cottages that housed three dozen
live-in servants.

Schley also built a pagoda-style watchtower south of his estate at the
top of Mount Prospect (later known as Schley Mountain), not far from
where the scenic overlook on Route 78 east of the Route 287 interchange
is today.

As 512 descends into Far Hills, you can still see evidence of the
Schley estate. Beside the rock walls are several Oriental monuments near
the roadside. The original indoor tennis court and stable buildings still
stand, and there is a big Spanish villa built by a subsequent generation.
The annual steeplechase at Moorland Farms attracts about forty thousand people who, for one day, get an inside look at the life of what's left
of the landed gentry and the equestrian set. And who, for one day, get to

be like them and walk the gently hilly property and take in the long vistas of the Somerset Hills.

Not all of the Schley estate remained as pristine. Two landmark symbols of suburban sprawl—the giant AT&T headquarters on Route 202-206 and the behemoth fifty-three-hundred-unit housing complex called The Hills in Pluckemin—are built on former Schley property.

Route 512, however, does not expose you to that. Instead, you duck north on Peapack Road into the village of Far Hills (built by Schley, who convinced the railroad to go that far west), past the wood frame Victorian in-town homes, past the park with its odd grandstand, past the Kate Macy Ladd estate, a three-story, forty-seven-room Tudor mansion set on a hill. Built in 1906 by the Macy's heiress and her husband, Walter Graeme Ladd, the property was willed to be maintained as a convalescent home for working women for fifty years after Ladd's death. In 1983, the home was bought by King Hassan II of Morocco. The king died in 1999, but the property remains in royal family hands.

The main entrance to Blairsden, another Somerset Hills turn-of-the-last-century stone mansion, is further up the road in Peapack-Gladstone. Blairsden has attracted its share of attention in the last few years. First, the order of nuns that owns it put it up for sale for $9 million, and an insurance group, headed by a guy now in federal prison, decided to buy it and turn it into a corporate retreat. The deal never materialized. Then a Somerset Hills group called the Blairsden Association got together with a plan to buy the mansion, restore it for a museum and cultural center (available for cocktail events), and keep the grounds as open space. The problem? The most state Green Acres funding they can possibly get is $500,000; the roads to the mansion aren't exactly built for public access; and the few neighbors—including the Matheny School, for children with severe muscular disorders—have indicated they may not appreciate the scotch-and-water crowd trying to wheel their way down the skinny mountain road in the dark. The police share those concerns. And the police have enough problems with Blairsden.

The mansion has always been a minor trespassing magnet for area teenagers and young adults, but in 1999, after the newsletter "Weird New

25. The moss-covered entrance to Blairsden off 512.
Photo by Mark Di Ionno.

Jersey" listed the by-then-vacant mansion as haunted, the situation got out of control. Kids from all over started showing up, and police say some vandalized the mansion and grounds. Municipal court judge Daniel Murphy, sitting in Peapack-Gladstone, hit each teen with the highest allowable fine of $352, which slowed the flow.

The mansion is still for sale as of this writing, and Pat Ryan of Turpin Realty told the *Star-Ledger* in July of 2000 she was showing the mansion two or three times a week. "It is probably the most popular property we have," she said.

Built in 1902 by financier C. Ledyard Blair for $2 million—at a time when a tenth of that would have built a near-palace—Blairsden was a sixty-thousand-square-foot Beaux Arts masterpiece, an ostentatious monument to the burgeoning wealth of the day and the area.

The architects were John Morven Carrere and Thomas Hastings, designers of the New York Public Library. The Italian gardens, waterfalls, and reflecting pools, surrounded by busts of Roman emperors, were designed by James Greenleaf, creator of the Lincoln Memorial.

Blair built a small railroad to the top of his mountain to transport building materials. The thirty-eight-room French Chateau has an indoor pool, squash courts, and Turkish baths. That is just the basement. The billiards-room walls are lined in leather, there is a large safe built into the kitchen pantry for the family silverware and Tiffany china. There are twenty-eight fireplaces, each with a hand-carved stone mantel made by Italian artisans brought to America for the job. A hand-painted mosaic round-stone path goes from the terraced yards down to the lake. Blair died in 1949, and the estate and surrounding four-hundred twenty-three acres of prime Somerset Hills real estate was put up for sale for a mere $250,000, a fraction of the building costs.

In a deal that makes you want to invest in the building of a time machine, the estate eventually sold at auction to an order of nuns. The Sisters of St. John the Baptist got the land and house—complete with all furnishings—for $60,000! God bless 'em.

For the next fifty years the nuns stayed there, and the great estate—long a social center for the Somerset Hills rich—became isolated, spooky, and shrouded in mystery.

I discovered Blairsden while exploring the backroads of Bernardsville and Mendham Township—narrow banked country lanes with names like Ballantine and Roebling and Dryden, named after the area's first-team capitalists—finding the vistas from hilltops like Mine Mountain and Mount St. John. I loved getting lost back there, driving aimlessly up the hills, along the linden tree-lined roads, looking at the old country estates. Each place was so different. Some were built to be seen, magnificent centerpieces of cleared-out property surrounded by well-maintained gardens. Others were built to be hidden, visible only in fall or winter through the bare trees, or low-roofed and tucked away from the road behind artificial walls or natural hillside barriers. Each had a story, a history to unlock. These were places built by somebodys, names recognized in the *Wall Street Journal* kind of way.

26 and 27. Blairsden, built by C. Ledyard Blair, one of the most ostentatious mansions of its day.
Star-Ledger photo by Joe Epstein (above); *Star-Ledger* photo by Tony Kurdzuk (below).

The scenery was not only beautiful but so far removed in character from the suburbs that a trip out there was like a drive through the English countryside. In the case of Blairsden—with its imposing roofline appearing through the trees, looming over the long and narrow deep basin of Ravine lake—it was like coming upon some Bavarian castle in the Black Forest.

Finding it, finding the way up to it—never to harm but to stand in awe—became a great adventure. And a great place to bring girls—parking on the closed gravel road over the Ravine Lake dam, hopping the brick wall with the mounted stone lion's head, circumventing the old rusting gate, sneaking up the round-stone path or along the paths through the woods, getting as close as you could without being detected. Coming upon the house, which rose up out of the woods, above the terraced lawns, a spectacle of wealth like something out of the movies. The weirdness of it all. The Roman-emperor heads, a lone old nun in dark blue sitting in a lawn chair. The quiet, near deserted ghost of a mansion.

I remember pressing forward, nudging and reassuring. Hands tightening on my arm as we neared closer to the home. Heartbeats quickened at the prospect of going someplace we shouldn't. Whispers, as if that somehow made you invisible.

"What if we get caught?"

"Don't worry . . . don't worry."

Co-conspirators. Sharing secrets. Finding a place to be alone. A place nobody would believe existed. A place where your imagination could run. Someday, this could be all yours. All of it, the house, the girl, the view of the rolling hills, a look into the future through a misty lens clouded by youth and hope, and the heavy, still air breathed only by trees.

All of this is what Route 512 means to me.

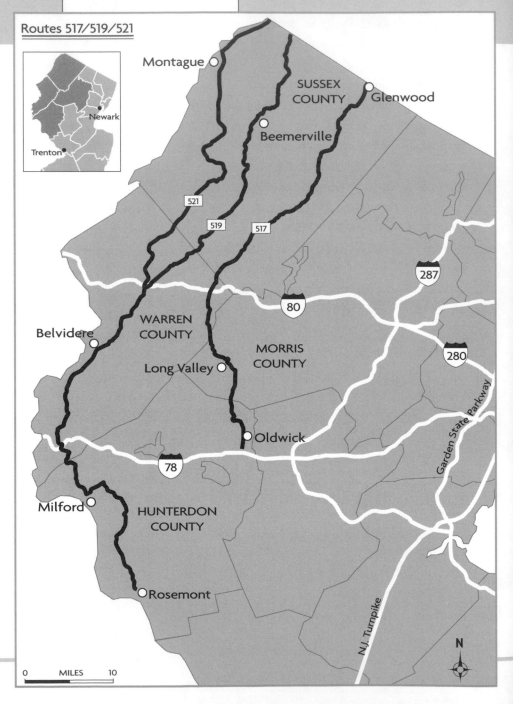

Routes 517/519/521

Montague

SUSSEX
COUNTY

Glenwood

Newark

Trenton

Beemerville

521

519

517

287

80

WARREN
COUNTY

Belvidere

MORRIS
COUNTY

280

Long Valley

Oldwick

78

Garden State Parkway

Milford

HUNTERDON
COUNTY

Rosemont

N.J. Turnpike

N

0   MILES   10

I was about ten years old, standing on the Pennsylvania side of the Delaware Water Gap, looking across Mount Tammany, the bigger bicep of the two mighty peaks there (see color plate 21).

My father was pointing to the craggy outcrops of quartzite, spiked at forty-five degree angles through the mountain, directing me to where they cut a naked, angular profile against the sky.

"You see the outline of the rocks?" he said, drawing lines in the air. "They make an Indian head."

I didn't see it.

"See, there's the brow, the nose, the chin . . . see it?"

I still didn't see it.

He tried again.

"Oh, yeah!" I lied. "Now, I see."

My father was satisfied: something taught, something learned, another trip worth taking.

It was that day, I think, or maybe another, that we had a catch with a football down by the river. There were other days at the gap—family picnics, wading in the Delaware, minor hiking, canoeing, and camping with the Boy Scouts. Each time, my father would point to that Indian head, and each time, the image would evade me.

About twenty-five years later, I parked in the same spot with my wife, Sharon, after a daylong ride through West Jersey. Life was pretty good. We shared a little rented house and had a Volkswagen Cabriolet convertible and while we were far from secure—I was somewhat in between jobs—we were happily pitching headfirst into our future. I remember thinking, could this really be me driving? Could I be this lucky in love?

Maybe it was because of my adult height, or my accumulation of life experiences, but my perspective had changed. Looking up at Mount Tammany that day, I saw, for the first time, the Indian head outlined in the rocks. I pointed it out to Sharon, and told her the story about my father.

" . . . and there it is," I said. "The old man was right."

That was a decade ago.

While I was writing this chapter, Sharon and I came east through the gap from Pennsylvania on one of those clear, low-humidity summer nights when the heat from the day is extinguished before the sun completely disappears.

The Cabriolet was long gone. In the back of our Chevy minivan were our four children, eight and under, whipped from an all-day family party. Three were asleep—only the older boy was awake, stubbornly fighting off sleep as sure as the twilight sky was holding off the night.

As we came through the gap, I wanted to say something about the Indian head, as I had every time we came through the gap, but I, too, was whipped and decided instead to value the silence.

"That looks like a waterfall," said a groggy voice from the back.

"What, Matt?" Sharon asked.

"The mountain up there. When you're looking at it sideways, it looks like a waterfall."

"You're right, Matt, it does look like a waterfall," his mother said. "It's like the clouds. You can see in it whatever you want."

Indian, waterfall, whatever, the one thing we all see at the gap is the sheer magnitude of its aeons-crafted beauty. The gap is a natural wonder, no different than other ancient, titanic rock formations of the Northeast—Niagara Falls, the cliffs of the Palisades, the Adirondack peaks, Mt. Washington in New Hampshire, the boulder-strewn Maine coast north of Bar Harbor. The gap is confirmation of New Jersey's great outdoors—the place to bring out-of-staters who think all New Jersey looks and smells like the Bayway Refinery area of the Turnpike. (Say this: judging all New Jersey by the Turnpike is like judging all California by East Los Angeles. It's not only unfair, but it shows true ignorance of geography.)

Pardon me if this sounds a little defensive, but I have traveled extensively through most of the country and seen many of its astounding natural wonders. I have also seen the underwhelming side—the grimy cities separated by miles and miles of boring flat countryside, a farm here and a farm there, a housing cluster here and a strip mall there, the scene playing out over and over, like miles ticking off an odometer. I have driven the eternal dullness of the interstate system, and negotiated the crash-zones of the state highways filled with the same chain plastic roofs of fast-food places and hotels, roads filled with K-Marts and Wal-Marts and every other regional "mart."

I admit that nothing in New Jersey has the God-sculpted hugeness and rainbow of earth tones of the Grand Canyon, or the heaven-bound ranges of the Rockies, or the angry, hellish, orange and red painted deserts and rock formations of the west. But east of the Continental Divide, we hold our own—not only in natural beauty but in *character*, as I hope the previous chapters in this book illustrate.

And no roads illustrate this better than Routes 517, 519, and 521, the three intercounty roads that travel hill and dale in the northwest part of the state, through New Jersey's mountain region. All three (along with 511 and 513 farther east) run on a northeast to southwest slant, following the ridge-and-valley pattern of the New Jersey Highlands.

These are driver's roads. Mostly open, curving, sloping—a gear-changing wind through New Jersey's most dramatic scenery, roads that are challenging and fun even when you keep the speed limit. Roads built for motorcycles and sporty car commercials. (I have spent the last few years banging along these roads in a Chevy pickup truck, and what I've lost in handling I've gained in view from the added height. Even in such a boat, with the windows open and the air rushing in, the roads feel like freedom.)

Route 517 has its beginnings in exurbia in the village of Oldwick, which looks like it sounds: a scrubbed little hamlet of elegant Victorian

28. Northern Warren County farm on 521.
Photo by Mark Di Ionno.

homes, with estates old and new perched on the surrounding hills. From Oldwick, 517 forms a sixty-mile arc starting in the wealth-belt hills of eastern Hunterdon and western Morris counties, going over Schooley's Mountain and through the Hackettstown area, into rural Sussex to the mountainous Vernon resort region.

While 519 and 521 are still mostly country roads, 517, in some places, is a road in transition, a line of demarcation between suburbia and true rurality. About one-half the road lies between Interstates 78 and 80—and the build-up, while not overwhelming, does lead to culture clash.

The Roehrich family has operated a dairy farm off 517 in Washington Township for two generations. Their black-and-white registered Holsteins graze in a pasture right across the street from Hastings Square—a 1980s "smart-growth" townhome and shopping development of about three hundred units.

Melinda Burdge, one of the Roehrich daughters, once told me she sees an uneasy coexistence between the two lifestyles.

"I've lived here my whole life and have seen a lot of changes, but the people don't always understand the realities of farming," she said a few years back. "They get mad when you tie up traffic, but there are times when you have to take a tractor out on the road. We also hear complaints about the way the cows smell or the way they look."

Another sign of the changing culture is in the rehab of old buildings. All along 517, many of the Gothic, Victorian, and colonial farmhouses and barns have been restored as private homes and businesses; the disrepair and neglect of old homes evidenced on more western and southern rural roads doesn't apply to the lower part of 517, a stretch where "country charm" has supplanted rural reality.

Nowhere is this more apparent than Long Valley, where 517 crosses 513 in the middle of the town. The village, settled by Germans in the mid-1700s and known as German Valley until World War I, is a collection of stone houses, mills, and barns turned into antique shops, professional offices, and restaurants.

And how's this for a uniquely American story? Right near a road marker that explains "Historic German Valley, est. 1750s . . . " and right behind old Nietzer's Tavern (c. 1750) which is now called Tavern Antiques, is a restored stone barn built in colonial America by German immigrants. The barn today is a restaurant, and the sign outside says "Hunan Wok of Long Valley (est. 1989)."

Just beyond the intersection of 517 and 513, just after 517 crosses the South Branch of the Raritan and before it climbs Schooley's Mountain, is a right-hand turn called Maple Street. Maple takes you past the Old Union Church ruins and cemetery. The ruins of the church, built in 1774, are the corners of all four walls, made of mortared fieldstone, which stand with soldierly straightness like some colonial Stonehenge. The graveyard headstones mark the passing of generations of families that date back to the earliest settlers, with names like the Duffords and the Flachs. One marker in particular echoes in the long-gone poetic language of the day:

Beneath this humble Monument
slumbers in humble ruins
the ashes of Ephraim Wells,
who exchanged this life
for immortality on April 17th, 1813,
aged 26 years.
"Ah! while we weep we sink
and we are what we deplore."

The road up Schooley's Mountain (elev. 1,073 feet) is winding and steep; treacherous coming down. The mountaintop community at one time was secluded and distant from the town below—a Jersey version of a West Virginia *holler*.

Nothing remains of the once-famous Schooley's Mountain springs, legendary among Native Americans for their healing powers and later the focal point of a large resort.

"When they decided to modernize the road to Hackettstown (517) back in the twenties, they blasted all along up there and ruined the spring," Virginia Allen, a Long Valley historian, once told me. At the crest of the hill is one remnant of the old town—the little general store, which dates back to the 1830s and also houses the village post office.

Going into Hackettstown, 517 crosses, then runs with, the Musconetcong River, sourced from Lakes Hopatcong and Musconetcong some twelve miles to the northeast.

Hackettstown is a Federalist-period town, and many of the old buildings are brick. In Hackettstown 517 joins Route 57 and then Route 46—a stretch that is becoming congested and overbuilt, with all the usual suspects, fast food, box stores, and strip malls. But a quick detour down any side street toward Centenary College will bring you into a large historic district, where the ornate college administration building stands as the centerpiece. This part of Hackettstown is shady and peaceful, and the restored Victorians rival the down-the-road collection in Oldwick. Route 517 breaks away from Route 46 in Hackettstown center and heads north and up, climbing in elevation toward Allamuchy. Here there is more evidence of the suburban-rural dichotomy: Panther Valley, another "smart-growth" complex of single- and attached-housing units, is fronted by a strip mall, hotel, and business center, all in architectural agreement in a country motif. Behind Panther Valley are an old horse farm and a series of side streets of old homes that reflect *authentic* rural ramshackle.

At the junction of 517 and Interstate 80 is a hill crest that shows off a view of the Delaware Water Gap—Mount Tammany on the Jersey side and Mount Minsi on the Pennsylvania—and the surrounding rounded hills of the Highlands. East of 517 is Allamuchy Mountain (elev. 1,222 feet), and the lush and expansive state park around it is always worth a side trip. The road north of here becomes more rugged as 517 cuts northeast through Sussex County, up through Sparta to another of Jersey's natural wonders—the mineral deposits of the Odgensburg-Franklin area.

The Highlands mishmosh of sedimentary, metamorphic, and igneous rock—some as old as the earth, and some laid down or spit out over the next 4.5 billion years—holds the most exotic and esoteric mineral deposits in the world. In all, over three hundred mineral varieties are found in the region, more than in any other discovered spike in the world. Of those, about 10 percent are unique to the region and some, like Franklinite (an iron-manganese-zinc oxide), are named in the area vernacular. Another twenty are radioactive, and many more are fluorescent, meaning they glow in the dark when hit with ultraviolet light. These rocks glow with colors so deep they could only have been mixed by millions of years of nature.

There were significant mining operations in the area during the eighteenth century, and the Franklin Mineral Museum and Sterling Hill Mining Company Historic Museum in Ogdensburg tell the history.

It was on one trip up 517 that I met Marj of Marj's Rock Shop in Franklin. Marj's Rock Shop was little more than a basement collection, with the obligatory black room for the fluorescence, but she sold mineral-encrusted rocks and opened her basement to whoever caught her at home. Marj had a good number of the metals and stones the area mines yielded—bits of gold, silver, and copper and pieces of sapphire, ruby, opal, tourmaline, quartz, smoky quartz, garnet, and zircon—all in bins for sale and under display lights.

"It's something I got interested in later in life," said Marj, about eighty at the time.

Marj did no advertising, except for a red-and-white lettered sign outside her home that simply said "Rock Shop," and she did not want her last name used in an article I wrote for the *Star-Ledger*.

"I have my regular customers, and they know where to find me," she told me. "Of course, if someone sees the sign and wants to stop in, that's okay, too. But if I put my last name in the paper, I know what will happen. My phone will start ringing off the hook, with people wanting to see the rocks. I can't have that. I need time for myself."

The last time I was up that way, I noticed the sign was gone, and so, I presumed, was Marj's Rock Shop.

Routes 519 and 521 can be traveled as a loop—a 140-mile asphalt lasso that captures the best rugged scenery of the state.

In itself, 519 may be the most scenic road of substantial length in New Jersey (see color plate 22).

Back in the days before I became an editor (rhymes with prisoner), I traveled the West Jersey "500" roads extensively in search of feature stories. These wind-whipped trips—some of them done as pleasure disguised as business in the convertible—were always productive.

Along Route 519 I found some of my favorite Jersey stories.

Among them:

THE SUSSEX VOLCANO

At the By-Acres dairy farm off 519 in Beemerville, cows climb a big hill behind the barn to graze lazily in the morning sun. But a couple of million years ago, the hill was a caldron of turbulence and upheaval, the hottest spitting violence the earth can muster. The big hill is the neck of a defunct volcano—one of only two in the state (the other being Fraternity Rock off the Turnpike in Secaucus)—and a real geologic oddity, according to Rutgers professor Michael Carr.

"There is a very rare type of magma there," Carr said. "Of the thousand or so active volcanoes in the world, only one has magma that has the same chemistry as Beemerville and I believe it's in South Central Africa."

Carr said the unusual rock is called carbonatite—a mixture of calcium and sodium carbonate.

"It's like a molten limestone," he said.

THE WORLD'S LARGEST BEAR

Goliath, a Kodiak bear, was the main attraction at Space Farms zoo on 519 in Beemerville.

"He was the biggest bear ever, that's a fact," said Fred Space, the zoo proprietor, who built the backyard animal menagerie kept by his father, a state trapper, into one of New Jersey's largest zoos (see color plate 23).

Goliath came to Space Farms in 1967 as a seventy-five-pound cub, bought from a zoo in Anchorage, Alaska. Over the years he grew to twelve feet tall and over a ton in weight—fully four feet taller and a thousand pounds heavier than the average Kodiak. *The Guinness Book of World Records* listed Goliath as not only the world's biggest bear but the heaviest carnivore ever.

When Goliath died in 1991, Fred Space went ahead with plans to preserve him.

"He was a remarkable specimen and we just didn't want to go out and put him in the ground somewhere," Space said.

So Goliath was mounted, and he stands in an eternal full-height taxidermic pose at the zoo's main entrance.

"People still come to see him," Space said. "They still look at him in awe."

THE CANAL MAN

Like many people born in the early twentieth century, Jim Lee knew people who lived in pretech times, people who had no machines, no phones, no electricity. Lee knew people like the canallers who captained boats pulled by mules along extensive artificial waterways, bringing crops, raw goods, and other material to the ports and markets of the East Coast. The canals of the Northeast—the Erie, the Delaware and Raritan, the Morris—were engineering feats, hand-dug rivers with lock systems called inclined planes that could float the big boats up and down mountains.

When Jim Lee was a boy, the people who worked the canals were already old, a dying breed. He heard their stories at a cigar store in Phillipsburg, where they spent their remaining days talking about the old times.

"I made up my mind right then and there to perpetuate their memory and the memory of the canal," Lee said. In 1946, Lee bought the old plane tender's house off 519 outside Phillipsburg and began to discover canal artifacts on the property, things like boat stoves, mule harnesses, and currency dating to 1861, which had been issued by the Morris Canal and Banking Company for use as legal tender along the canal. He became the leading authority on the canal and wrote two books about it. His house became a virtual museum of canal tools and equipment and paper memorabilia.

Then in 1971 he unearthed the giant turbine wheel, installed in 1850, that made the inclined plane work—but not before removing tons of rocks and debris that had been thrown into the thirty-four-foot well where the wheel was housed. The wheel was restored, not quite to working order, but enough to look the way it did one hundred and fifty years ago.

THE WINDMILL IN HOLLAND *(as in the township)*

The late Poul Jorgensen was a ship's engineer in Holland (the country) and a tool-and-die maker in America. When he retired in the early sixties, he decided to build a windmill as a working monument to the human ingenuity behind the centuries-old milling process.

Jorgensen visited windmills all over Europe, doing architectural drawings. Then he started building. Twenty years later, he completed his fully operational, seven-story grain mill, which still sits high atop a wind-whipped hill off Adamic Hill Road, just off 519.

Jorgensen opened his windmill to the public, but died a few years after it was completed. His nephew, Charles Brown, is now responsible for maintaining the mill and keeping it open.

"He was an amazing guy," said Brown. "When you look at the engineering complexity of this thing, and the amount of heavy labor that went into it, well, it's really a remarkable achievement."

THE DAVISES' LOTS OF TIME SHOP

In Rosemont, the Davises have had an antique and clock-repair store for nearly forty years (see color plate 24). Their little weathered bungalow of a building was once a blacksmith shop, then an office for a chicken hatchery.

While the Lots of Time Shop seems out of the way, proprietor Tim Davis says you'd be surprised at who pops in. "My grandmother put out a guest book for people to sign. By 1978, she had people from all fifty states and seven countries. I assume we have people from more countries by now."

Davis says one reason people find him is because "we're less than a mile from the last covered bridge in New Jersey, which is on Route 604 between here and Sergeantsville. So we get a lot of people who want to sightsee in this area. Of course, we also get the people who come in and say, 'I'm lost. Where am I?'"

Route 519 begins near Rosemont just north of Stockton in lower Hunterdon County, and runs along the mountaintops that overlook the Delaware River valley. Like many places along 519, Stockton is a town out of New Jersey's back pages. I remember driving through one morning and coming upon a Rockwellian scene at the town's little blue school-house on Route 29: As the children filed into class, a boy, still-wet hair plastered against his head, leaned out of a second-floor window and fitted the American flag snugly into its holder above the entranceway. Naturally, I was without a camera. I missed another photo op the next time through. This time it was a group of older adults—presumably part of a seniors drawing class at the Prallsville Mill arts center in Stockton—sitting in a line of chairs under a tree on a knoll, all sketching the scenic, riverside mill.

From Rosemont, 519 connects a series of little villages—Kingwood, Baptistown, Palmyra, Everittstown—before hooking down to Milford.

In each of these little villages are a collection of nineteenth-century houses and a church of some Protestant denomination with a roadside cemetery. These are backroads towns, and this is rural New Jersey. Most of it is charming, but some of it isn't too pretty.

Each village has its share of modest restored Victorian homes, and others that have been neglected to the point of ruin. Each has its antique shops, some selling "finds," some selling other people's junk. Each has its general stores, some converted into nouveau cuisine restaurants, others where you can still buy bread, milk, mothballs, and a cold Dr. Pepper, and still others that have been shut down. In Alexandria, the wooden Greek Revival bank at the center of town is closed and for sale. Outside every one of these towns are a few abandoned barns and other

29. Downtown Alexandria, Route 519 in Hunterdon County.
Photo by Mark Di Ionno.

30 and 31. Rural dilapidation along 519.
Photos by Mark Di Ionno.

32. Greenwich housing development near Route 22 in Warren County.
Photo by Mark Di Ionno.

farm outbuildings about to collapse, evidence of the dying agricultural way of life in these parts. The raggedness of these sagging human-built structures, with their hundred-year shelf life, is a sharp contrast to nature's backdrop—the rounded green hills, the meadows of swaying field grass, the long-distance views of softened colors in summer's humid air, the eternal stillness of the space.

This scenery stays with you most of the way, through Milford, Spring Mills, and Riegel Ridge and as the road nosedives down through the Musconetcong Valley. Only near the intersection with Route 22 in Warren County do you run into suburban sprawl on 519—traffic lights, shopping centers, and a series of new, single-family housing developments.

From there to north of Belvidere, 519 hooks around a Highlands ridge network mostly called Upper Pohatcong Mountain. The ridge is a series of rounded peaks called Scotts Mountain (elev. 1,093 feet), Mount No More (elev. 1,150), Oxford Mountain (953), County House Mountain (1,157), Mount Mohepinoke (1,145), High Rock Mountain (675), Danville

Mountain (1,135), and Jenny Jump Mountain (1,134). The ridge is to the east of 519, and to the west there is a long, flat valley which is nearly level with the Delaware River. The power plant that looms over it is actually in Pennsylvania.

Agriculture is still strong in this area, although some farms are in transition. Wineries, Christmas-tree farms, and pick-your-own gardens have replaced the truck farms of yesteryear, where corn and other vegetables were grown, transported, and sold in bulk. Still, the natural beauty hasn't changed. The road curves through these farms, following the contours of the hilly landscape above the farmers' fields where, on a summer night, thickly swarming lightning bugs flirt with the plant tops, carpeting the valley with their glow.

Just south of Hope, the terrain becomes more rocky and the farmscape turns bovine. Dairy farms with black-and-white Holsteins are spread out over endless acres. There are beef cattle, too, red Herefords and Black Angus, huddling together along fences or under shade trees.

The rock-strewn landscape has made its mark on architecture, too. Around Hope, stone houses and barns become more commonplace. Hope itself, settled and built by Moravian colonists who came east from Bethlehem, Pennsylvania, in 1774, is a village of structures made mostly of blue limestone. Hope is picturesque, but because of its proximity to Route 80 many of those restored blue limestone structures now house real-estate offices. Hope is no longer rural, it's exurban—a wealth-belt town clinging to (some may call it commercially exploiting) its country charm.

A truer rural hamlet is just north in Johnsonburg. Like the villages along the Hunterdon County part of the road, Johnsonburg has its contrasts. Across the street from the town cemetery with its rusting gate is a beautifully restored masonry octagonal house, one of only a few in New Jersey. Up the street from the octagonal house are a number of small, dilapidated bungalows, with junked autos and appliances rusting in the yards.

As 519 heads into Sussex County the rock becomes shale, and there are a number of small quarrying operations on the road. The terrain also

33 and 34. Rural
scenes on 519 in
Warren County.
Photos by
Mark Di Ionno.

35. The Octagonal House in Johnsonburg.
Photo by Mark Di Ionno.

becomes more mountainous as the road cuts through the Highlands. Here 519 goes through the valleys and foothills of the Kittatinnys, passing through Newton, then Branchburg and Beemerville, both in the shadow of Sunrise Mountain (elev. 1,653 feet). The road runs parallel to the Appalachian Trail through here, staying in the valley below the famed hiking trail, then exiting the state just south of High Point State Park.

High Point State Park is—in effect, not literally—where 519 and 521 come back together.

The two roads first intersect down in Hope center—519 turns east, and 521 heads west. Where 519 stays rural, 521 goes rugged. The road goes to Blairstown, then runs along the Paulins Skill, through the White Lake Wildlife Management Area to Stillwater, and swings around the green-shuttered First Presbyterian Church, a squat Gothic structure in mint condition. At Middleville there is a classic confrontation of rural versus suburban: an old-fashioned, weathered general store is right across the street from a new upscale storefront restaurant that promises fine dining. The general store sells bait (I'll pass on jokes about French food being bait dressed in a béchamel sauce), and this part of the road is the entrance to North Jersey's hunting and fishing paradise. Swartswood Lake and Little Swartswood Lake appear off 521, lakes shared equally by bathers, boaters, and fishers.

At Myrtle Grove, 521 turns left and climbs four hundred feet toward the Kittatinnys, through the Bear Swamp Wildlife Management Area, past the lake community of Crandon Lakes. The road then turns northeast and runs parallel with the mountain ridge as it passes the high Sussex lakes of Owassa and Culvers, which, like the Swartswoods, are big enough to accommodate all kinds of use. At Culvers Lake, 521 forms a ten-mile junction with Route 206, much of which runs through forested country set aside for open space and public use: Stokes State Forest and then the upper reaches of the Delaware Water Gap National Recreation Area. Just north of Culvers, the road intersects with the Appalachian Trail, and it is not unusual to see wild-looking backpacked hikers on their way to either Georgia or New Hampshire coming down off the mountain for supplies at a little store/way station.

When 521 breaks off again from Route 206 near the entrance to Milford-Montage Bridge, it becomes part of what may have been the Old Mine Road, built in the 1650s and locally claimed to be the oldest road in America. The Dutch built the road to explore mineral deposits, and found copper along the Delaware. The road they built stretched one hundred and forty miles from this region to Kingston, New York, where there was a bigger settlement. Here along 521 are a number of old stone houses dating back to the 1700s, some used as forts or barracks in the century-long series of skirmishes with the Indians.

The road goes into Port Jervis, New York, where it intersects with New York's Route 6. Less than a mile east, Route 6 intersects with New Jersey's Route 23, which will take you through High Point State Park and back to 519.

As this was being written, the High Point Monument was closed, undergoing extensive renovation. But when open, the two-hundred-twenty-foot obelisk atop the highest point of both the Kittatinnys and the state of New Jersey (elev. 1,803 feet), literally expands the horizon of New Jersey's natural beauty (see color plate 25).

"People always ask, 'How far can you see from the top of the monument?'" Tony Sappio, the chief ranger at High Point, once told me. "It's like looking up at the stars. How far away are they? From the top of the monument, you have unlimited visibility."

From the top of the monument, nearby Port Jervis looks like a toy city, something you might see on an elaborate miniature train set. The distant mountains of New Jersey, New York, and Pennsylvania seem painted against the sky, in infinite hues of blue, green, and purple. And if you look southwest, down the Kittatinny Ridge toward the Delaware Water Gap, everything you see belongs to you.

"That's all public land," said Sappio. "It's High Point [State Park], then Stokes [State Forest], then the federal park [the Delaware Water Gap National Recreation Area]. When you look down there, you know that land is going to be there for your grandchildren and their grandchildren."

This is my New Jersey.

The last time I went to the Gap, I parked on the Pennsylvania side, just as I had done with my dad so many years earlier.

From one of the stone-walled overlooks, I saw the Indian head, brow, nose, and chin, jutting against the sky. I saw the mountains come together, the layers of sheer and wooded rock towering over the wide green river. Down below a few canoeists moved silently, headed toward the mountain cleft, ready to disappear around the river bend.

I stood up on the wall and took a few pictures, and thought how I had shared this view with so many different people over the course of my life and how—God willing—I would share it in the future.

Just then a young couple parked and walked to the back corner of the wall. She was beautiful—tall, angular, and athletic, with strong Nordic features. He was, well, lucky in love, but clearly a romantic— appreciative of, and appreciated by, the young woman.

She sat on the wall and he leaned into her lap, both looking toward the mountains. I was struck by their sweetness toward one another, how easily they fell into one another and how naturally they fit together, just like the two mountains of the gap. They were in comfortable love— maybe forever, maybe not—but the memory they were creating for themselves, at that moment, in that setting, could be as eternal as the mountains in front of them, given the chance. They talked quietly, hands and arms and hips together in ways so innocent, I did not feel like an intruder. Instead, I shared their comfort, relaxing with them in the intimate setting, the imposing gap in the short distance giving us all reason to share the space without self-consciousness—the young lovers and the middle-aged guy with the camera—gathered there to admire its sheer rock and sheer magnitude. It was their place, it was my place . . . it belonged to anyone willing to be embraced by the beauty of the view. It can belong to you.

I left after a while, still thinking of the times I have shared that view.

Me, I have been the young man held in those arms, heart soaring like the eagles and hawks who glide effortlessly on the warm updrafts of air over the gap.

I've been the boy shielding his eyes against the sun, trying to make out the Indian profile against the glare, propped up on the rocks in the strong hands of his father.

I've been the father, pointing toward those mountains, saying, "Never let anyone tell you that you live in an ugly state."

Someday, I'll be the grandfather, handing down the legacy of the state's beauty and history to another generation, passing on the family love of this state and the desire to explore it.

Someday beyond that, when my reflexes are too dulled and my hands too shaky to control a car, when my eyes see little more than the shadows and my mind wanders through an attic of memories, I hope a son, daughter, or grandchild bundles me up and puts me in a car and rolls down the windows so I can feel the fresh air swirling around on my face, mussing my grayed, thinning hair. That sense of breezy movement has been as important to me as any of my other senses, a true guiding light of my life.

When I'm old, I hope someone cares enough to remember that. More than that, I hope they use "a ride with grandpop" as an excuse to wander for themselves, to let their restlessness lead them into their world, to let their restlessness always make that world seem new, to never tire of exploring it.

Until then, I will be behind the wheel, one eye on the road, one eye on the landscape, taking people to places where memories are made, and saying to whoever is along for the ride, "Hey, look . . . just over there. . . ."

MARK DI IONNO, an award-winning journalist, is the assistant managing editor, Local News, at the *Star-Ledger,* the largest-circulation newspaper in New Jersey. His first book, *New Jersey's Coastal Heritage: A Guide* (Rutgers University Press, 1996), won the New Jersey Studies Academic Alliance Award. Born and raised in New Jersey, Di Ionno now lives in Mountain Lakes. He is the father of six children, some of whom "kid-tested" the attractions in this book.